STEP OUT

and TAKE YOUR PLACE

"In one of the most authentic voices I have ever encountered, Krista delivers the encouragement, inspiration and tools to Step Out and Take Your Place. This book is for anyone who has ever struggled with finding and feeling strong purpose, asked "what now or what's next," or trembled over the question, "Who, me?" If you have wondered about your gifts or how to honor them with your life, this is your book. It is a blessing, beginning with page 1."

–Dondi Scumaci, Author of *Designed for Success: Ten Commandments for Women in the Work Place, Ready, Set...Grow,* and *Career Moves*

"Krista Dunk's journey with God will inspire you to settle for nothing less than God's plan. Her gentle spirit and strong word will invite you to grow in faith, and to step out and take your place in life."

–Jason Frenn, Bestselling Author and Missionary Evangelist, www.Frenn.org

"Krista Dunk is an inspiration to anyone who is interested in pursuing their goals. She inspires and encourages all who God places in her path. She has keen insight and a listening ear that brings comfort to anyone who may have doubts regarding the path God has chosen. I have had the honor and the privilege of being one of the souls Krista has touched with her spiritual resources. I appreciate what she has offered and what she is willing to continue to contribute to the success of my endeavors."

–Minister Inez Reilly, Author of *All Other Ground, Covenant* and *How To Taste It at the End of the Day*

"What an amazing resource! Step Out and Take Your Place is your A-Z guide for discovering and developing your unique, God-given life direction. Like having a compass in your hand, Krista's clear and actionable advice could change everything!"

–Marnie Swedberg, Mentor to Leaders, www.Marnie.com

"Krista, I love your passion, your focus, your examples, and your book is a timely answer to a heart-cry that often goes unanswered."

–Lois Williams, Author of *Heart Chords – Harmony in a Soul Set Free*

STEP OUT
and TAKE YOUR PLACE

How to Discover
and Live Your
Everyday Calling

Krista Dunk

WESTBOW
PRESS
A DIVISION OF THOMAS NELSON

WestBow Press books may be ordered through booksellers or by contacting:

WestBow Press
A Division of Thomas Nelson
1663 Liberty Drive
Bloomington, IN 47403
www.westbowpress.com
1-(866) 928-1240

Because of the dynamic nature of the Internet, any web addresses or links contained in this book may have changed since publication and may no longer be valid. The views expressed in this work are solely those of the author and do not necessarily reflect the views of the publisher, and the publisher hereby disclaims any responsibility for them.

Any people depicted in stock imagery provided by Thinkstock are models, and such images are being used for illustrative purposes only.

Certain stock imagery © Thinkstock.

ISBN: 978-1-4497-0639-5 (sc)
ISBN: 978-1-4497-1565-6 (dj)
ISBN: 978-1-4497-1583-0 (e)

Library of Congress Control Number: 2011926673

Printed in the United States of America

WestBow Press rev. date: 04/26/2011

Dedication & Acknowledgments

First and foremost, this book is dedicated to El Shaddai, the Almighty God. Without You, I am nothing and have nothing. This book is also dedicated to you, the reader. With God's direction, I wrote this book for you. My desire is to see you take this information and run with it.

A special thank-you to:

- ❋ My husband and children
- ❋ My parents and family
- ❋ All the KBWomen business ladies
- ❋ Friends who have encouraged me
- ❋ The leaders at Capital Christian Center
- ❋ Friends who inspire me by sharing their gifts

Table of Contents

Foreword
by Pastor Dave Minton

One of the greatest days of my life was when I realized that God gifted me for public speaking. It wasn't something that I was really preparing to do in my life, until one day I found myself in a situation where I was speaking to a group of people. All of a sudden, this new confidence came out of me! I've always been a shy guy and someone that you would see sitting in the back of the room, not in the front. When I realized that God had placed a gift in me to communicate and teach, it was truly a turning point in my life.

"A man's gift makes room for him, and brings him
before great men." – Proverbs 18:16 (NASB)

Tapping into the gift of public speaking really changed my life. It took shyness and lack of confidence and replaced it with courage and faith. As I'm serving others with the gift that God has given me, it has allowed me to see God work in such an amazing way in my life; also bringing encouragement, wisdom, and inspiration to others.

Krista and her new book have really hit a homerun! ***Step Out and Take Your Place*** is a guide to taking practical steps in developing your everyday calling. I encourage you to discover the gifts that God has placed in you. It is one of the greatest things you can ever do for yourself!

So get ready to go on a journey of discovery and step out in your calling. Live the full life of the gifts that God has called you to.

Dave Minton
Senior Pastor
Capital Christian Center
Olympia, WA
www.Go2CCC.org

Preface

Circus day had finally arrived! As a six-year-old coloring contest winner, I had anticipated this day for weeks. Oh the tremendous pride I felt about winning tickets for my whole family, and for all the hard, meticulous coloring work I had done on that entry paper. Winning the contest also meant we were able to bring an extra guest with us that day - a student from my father's 5th grade class also joined us. I even had a special winner's hat to wear to the event to signify my special status.

I was nervously excited as we stepped into the massive, colorful tent. Being a very shy child, I clung to my parents, and spoke to no one as we weaved our way through to our seats. It was a noisy and crowded place, filled with people, animals, popcorn, and balloons. We found our seats, and I bubbled with excitement, awaiting the start of the show.

As the circus show started, the crowd buzzed and roared with each new act and performance. It was all fun and games (literally) until they made an announcement over the PA system; an announcement I was not expecting. "Would the coloring contest winners please join us in the center ring."

Oh no…I suddenly realized they were talking about me. That announcement was horrifying. My heart sank, and began to beat wildly. My eyes darted around the tent at all the people, at the center ring, at my parents. All those eyes looking at me? Go out *there*? "No, I don't want to go!" I refused to leave my seat. A last call rang out over the loudspeakers…it was my last chance to go out. I stayed firmly planted in my seat and was not budging.

My parents didn't want to force me out there, yet didn't want the opportunity to be wasted either. My little sister was too young to go, but the guest student we brought with us seemed thrilled at the idea to get up and take part in the festivities. They gave her the okay, and I was relieved to be off the hook. "Problem solved," I thought, with a deep sigh. I did not have to suffer that *horrible embarrassment*.

She quickly stood up, my parents handed her my winner's hat and then she hurried down the stairs and out into the ring.

To this day, I remember the feeling of great regret as I watched my dad's student run down the steps, with my hat on, into the center ring, to take part in my reward. That was my place! That was my honor and privilege! I earned that! It was mine! I suddenly longed to be out there, but I had already made my choice to reject it. It was too late.

My own timidity stopped me from receiving what was rightfully mine. I refused to step out and take my place.

This experience was a defining moment in my young life. After decades had gone by, God reminded me of it to get a glimpse at how easily we miss the good plan He has for us and reject what is rightfully ours. This story from my past is the reason why this book is called *"Step Out and Take Your Place."*

How many of us haven't stepped out and taken our place, and we knew it was ours?

Conversely, how many of us do not even know what place to step in to yet?

Greetings, friend. My name is Krista Dunk, the author of this book, and I would like to share my heart with you for a few moments. I want to tell you how my life has completely transformed, since I took a journey with God to discover His plan for my life. I can now step out and take my place because I've discovered what place that is, and have renewed my mindset about who I am.

Even though I was a believer in God, for many years, my life was routine, predictable and small. I suffered with timidity and an inability to express myself effectively. At the same time, at the core of me, I knew there was an underlying level of dormant destiny. It caused me to have an unsettled, frustrated feeling inside, leading me to search, grasp and experiment with many different career, ministry, educational, and business opportunities.

At some point in my thirties, I'd finally had enough. Trying to figure things out myself was not working. "Lord! I just want to be in Your will!

Help me figure out my life within Your master plan." That question, combined with wanting to know my personal potential, started my journey to seek God about His calling for my life.

For me, it's been a journey of struggle, revelation, peace, trust, renewal, change, and persistence. Becoming aware of God's everyday calling for me has been like a light switch with a dimmer. At first it was dark, then, gradually new levels of light have illuminated my surroundings as I've become more aware of who God created me to be and the work He has set before me.

I pray that you too will come out of the darkness, or areas of unrevealed wisdom, into the light and awareness of who you are at the core. God will finish the work he has started in you as you remain faithful and connected to Him.

Since God is my source, my promise to Him is this: Whatever He shows me, teaches me or speaks to me, I will turn around and share that wisdom with others. Writing *Step Out and Take Your Place* has stirred up many truths and lessons learned which I can now impart to you. In various ways, I myself am still moving through the journey described in this book.

While working through this book, my hope and dream for you is this:

- You go deeper in God and know Him more,
- You become aware of the gifts He has given you, and get a vision for His overall calling for your life, and
- You gain confidence and a renewed mindset, and are empowered to step out and take your God-ordained place.

Imagine a world in which everyone embarks on, and completes, a journey to find their God-given gifts, they understand God's plan for their lives and then they step out to take their places - every day, not just on Sundays. *That* is an exciting thought to me.

Maybe you feel small. Maybe you're unsatisfied with your daily grind. Maybe you're not sure you are in God's will for your life. Maybe you want to make a difference in the world. Maybe you've been living a random life, experimenting and complying with whatever opportunity comes by. Maybe you'd like to *Step Out and Take Your Place*, but are not sure where to start. Within this book, I have defined The Gift Discovery Cycle™ and

Calling Components™. As you keep reading, these and other processes will take you on a journey to discover for yourself all that you have been created for.

You probably already realize I'm not a world-famous person. I am not a pastor of a mega-church. I am not a biblical scholar with decades of education. I am a woman of God who has been transformed by God. If He can use *me*, if He can speak a message of hope that stirs you up to good works through *me*, I *know* He can use you. He uses regular, everyday people like you and I to make an impact!

> *"Then I told them of the hand of my God which had been good upon me; and also of the king's words that he had spoken to me. Then they said, 'Let us rise up and build.' So they strengthened their hands for this good work."* –Nehemiah 2:18 (KJV)

My desire is to see you discover and strengthen your hands for good work; the good work God has prepared for you. Your life, and the lives of those who you will impact, will never be the same.

I want you to give yourself permission to express the beautiful treasure within. What will it take for you to give yourself permission? Are you ready to take the journey to discover what God has placed within?

It is time for you to *Step Out and Take Your Place*!

Blessings,
Krista Dunk

www.StepOutandTakeYourPlace.com

Introduction

"How can I know that I am following God's will in my life?"
"I am not sure what my God-given gifts, talents and purpose in this life are."
"I can only see part of the puzzle."
"How do I trust God more and stop the fear?"

How do I know that others are searching for God's calling; searching for their place? I suspected that my experience was not uncommon, and my research proved it. Those statements and questions above are just a few of the many candid responses I received from the survey I did in 2010. I surveyed scores of Godly women (and some men too), asking them questions about their personal experiences and questions on this topic. I have found that most people lack clarity about their unique gifts and calling.

Sixty percent of the respondents did not even know one of the most basic gifts-related pieces of information about themselves; what their God-given spiritual gifts are. Mind you, these were church-going people!

Not only did I survey these Godly people, but I also interviewed pastors, ministers, Christian counselors, women's ministry directors, pastor's wives, etc. I wanted to know what they had experienced and seen in the people they work with who remain unaware of their God-given gifts and calling. I found that nearly all of them were deeply passionate about this topic too. Their hearts share the same cry for people to find their unique roles within God's purposes, which leads them to grow and flourish in life.

*"I keep asking that the God of our Lord Jesus Christ, the glorious Father, may give you the Spirit of wisdom and revelation, so that you may know him better. I pray also that the eyes of your heart may be enlightened in order that you may **know the hope to which he has called you**, the riches of his glorious inheritance in the saints, and his incomparably great power for us who believe."* – Ephesians 1:17-19 (NIV)

You may be asking, "What can I expect from this book? Will it be another book that tells me to find my gifts, but then leaves me still wondering how?"

Let me answer that now. In *Step Out and Take Your Place*, I'm going to accompany you on a journey to take you from frustration and searching, to seeking God and getting new revelation of who you are. Through stories, assessments, scriptures, tips, and practical examples you'll get new wisdom and helpful information on how to seek God and investigate yourself. You get the "how" and not just the "why."

Step Out and Take Your Place offers you an exciting, unique journey. Within the pages of this book, you will gain understanding in these areas:

- Recognize the need to find your gifts
- Get a clear, how-to path for discovering your gifts and calling
- Help in understanding the inner and outer work necessary to reach goals
- Explore how to develop and effectively share your gifts with the world
- Inspiration that motivates you to seek the heart of God
- Get clarity about your future

I know you want clarity, and may be tired of going with life's default flow. Maybe you are like I was, and you hop on every bandwagon, say yes to every opportunity and over commit yourself because you are searching for more.

The first step in getting clarity about your purpose and calling is to know who you are in Christ. Clarity about what your gifts are is step two. No more random life. No more feeling lost in the shuffle of activities. No more living in a small comfort zone that leaves you unfulfilled and frustrated.

The Gift Discovery Cycle™, outlined in this book, will show you the process of discovering what your gifts are. Spiritual gifts play a key role. However, God has created you with many other components that work together and that play a part in your overall calling.

You will be encouraged to renew your mind, and have your self-image match the image of who God sees you as. This is key; if you cannot believe and agree with God about His future for you, your own mind will self-sabotage your own destiny.

Along with having practical strategies to move forward with, there are several key perspectives I want you to walk away with as well. One example of these concepts is this:

- Your gifts and calling are not just for Sundays; they are in effect Monday through Saturday as well. The special piece you bring to the body of Christ is vital, and much needed, 24/7.

It's time to get ready start your journey of discovery.

Read on, and enjoy the journey!

Because of the detailed journey this book covers, you will receive the most benefit from having both this book, and the corresponding workbook. Please visit www.StepOutandTakeYourPlace.com for workbook information.

Get Ready

"For we are God's workmanship, created in Christ Jesus to do good works, which God prepared in advance for us to do." – Ephesians 2:10 (NIV)

1.
You Are Gifted

Deep inside, I have always known that God made me unique. I have held onto that truth from a young age. Even so, my dormant destiny lived in hiding alongside mediocrity and predictable, small living.

Everything felt scattered and unclear. I was one of God's people and yet had no idea what God's plan for my life was, and I didn't know how to find that information.

Today as I look back on my life, I recognize that an underlying frustration sprouted and grew. I was subtly frustrated about life; frustrated about not knowing my gifts; frustrated about not knowing the dreams God had for me. I desperately wanted to live within His will, but felt that I was falling short of that by not knowing His calling or plan for me.

Can you relate?

All people have a deep longing inside, a void that can only be filled by understanding why God has created them. "What is my purpose? What are my gifts and how can I use them?"

Believe me, I understand these heart cries very well. I wrote this book for you.

1

While in the process of seeking God about my gifts, and then about His overall plan and call for my life, the things He's shown me have been life changing. I want you to have the same joy and understanding for yourself. I want to see you discover your gifts and use them in a powerful way. By sharing my journey, experiences and course of action, I hope to provide you with insights that can help you discover your God-given gifts too. By telling my own story of struggle, small beginnings and breakthrough, I hope it also inspires and encourages you. The same can happen in your life!

Two significant life events have given me a completely new perspective on finding purpose and discovering my giftings from God. The first has to do with my family of origin. Let me give you some background.

Many generations of people in my family are singers. Not just my mom, dad and sister, but uncles, aunts, and grandparents too! And many are school teachers…Both of which, while growing up, I vowed I would never have anything to do with. The natural vocal talent to sing was there in my DNA (undeveloped), but the desire to use it was not.

At age twenty-two, I rededicated my life to Christ and started going to church again with my mom, step-father and sister. Soon after, my mother and sister talked me into joining the church choir, which was large and easy to "hide" in. And remember, I wasn't a center stage kind of girl, so hiding was key! It was actually fun, but at that point I was still doing it mostly out of a sense of obligation to my mother.

My mother and sister were the super-star singers, and I was proud of them. One day, however, they asked me the unthinkable; to sing in a trio. With a microphone? God-forbid! I'd never sung with a microphone before, and had barely ever picked one up in my lifetime. But the three of us regularly talk each other into doing stuff we'd prefer not to, so this request was no different. I reluctantly agreed.

We rehearsed for several weeks, and finally performance day came. My knees knocked and hands shook as we took the stage, microphones in hand. For my mother and sister, all of this was like second nature, but I had to force my feet forward one step at a time. I don't think I made eye contact with a single person in the congregation the whole time we sang. My lyric sheet was my shield!

We performed our song for two services that day, and it actually went very well. I felt simultaneously proud of myself and relieved. It was over!

About a month later, the whole family drove to visit my step-father's parents in a town about forty-five minutes away. Both of them were in their seventies and had serious health issues. It had been a long time since they'd been able to go anywhere other than doctors' offices. They were kind people, and always thrilled when we visited.

After lunch, my mother leaned over to my sister and me, and enthusiastically said, "We should sing them our song!" My shoulders slumped. That was not what I wanted to hear, or do for that matter.

"Oh man…no…seriously? Don't make me do it!" No sooner had those words escaped my lips, than this revelation came to my mind: "Your gift is not about you." So far, it had been all about me. Honestly, I didn't want to admit to having or owning this singing gift at all. I had pushed it away for years.

It was time to get over myself.
It was time to own it.
It was time to use what God gave me to bless others.
It was time to open my mouth and share it.

We sang our song for them and it gave them such tremendous joy. The image of the tears in their eyes and the joy on their faces still lives in my memory. That song was the only "church" they'd been able to have in months, and that day continues to be a lesson in humility. Since then, they have both passed away. I would have regretted not singing for them. By opening my mouth, I not only shared my God-given gift but also gave them a gift.

> *"But the plans of the LORD stand firm forever, the purposes of*
> *His heart through all generations." –* Psalm 33:11 (NIV)

The second perspective-shifting event happened about six months after my friend, Tammy Redmon, and I started an organization for faith-based women in business, called Koinonia Business Women (KBWomen). It was a vision from the Lord.

One Saturday morning as I was waking up, I was praying and talking to God silently in my mind. Our church was in the process of reading a book about purpose, and I had been meditating on that subject for about a week or so. At that moment, I was pondering how Koinonia Business Women existed in part to help women in business find their God-given plan.

Then it happened; God sent a Rhema word and a vision to my mind. In a flash, I saw a very thin, weak person standing alone. This very gaunt person with sunken features was alive, but totally lacking in any power or strength. The Rhema word audio message that God gave me along with the image was this: "Build up the body."

Just as the visual and audio flashed into my mind, so did their meaning: The body of Christ is weak and is merely surviving. God's people are lacking in the strength and power needed to take ground for the Kingdom. We are missing some kind of necessary nourishment.

It was time to build up the body, and apparently I had a role to play. The vision was astounding. It changed me.

If you knew me personally, it's slightly ironic that I could have a role to play in God's "build up the body" purposes. I've been a small, thin person all my life, who looks like I probably couldn't even break a kid's birthday party piñata if I needed to. Aside from that, I'm certainly not someone who is somehow more "qualified" to be used by Him than anyone else.

I thank God that He looks at a different kind of strength when He chooses people to do His work! Our physical strength does not qualify us. And for that matter, our formal education, fancy resumes or multiple titles behind our names don't either. We simply put on *His* power and strength.

> *"For it is not the one who commends himself who is approved, but the one whom the Lord commends."* – 2 Corinthians 10:18 (NIV)

Time after time in the scriptures, God uses anyone willing – not necessarily people of high position, experience, education or stature. Yes, we all have our own personal strengths, abilities, character flaws and weaknesses, but *God does not require perfection for service.*

You bring something special to the world that no one else can. God wants to speak to you and show you things about your gifts and your life's mission. You *are* gifted and called!

> God does not require perfection for service.

Summary

People have a deep desire to understand what they are meant to do and meant to be. Trying to discover this apart from God, will be a futile effort. Each person has been specifically created to play a role in His plan and purposes. He has a good work planned for you.

Some of us have rejected our gifts, only to find out that they are not for ourselves – they are for others. When using our God-given gifts, others are blessed and we are fulfilled.

God does not require prior qualifications or perfection for Him to use you. No matter who you are, He wants to show you things, give you experiences and revelations and speak to you about what He has for you. He may speak to you through dreams, visions, the Bible, another person, during worship, etc.

You are gifted and called!

Prayer: *Father God, You are all-powerful. Thank You for working all around me. Help me to understand in my heart that I am gifted and called according to Your purposes. Show me how my gifts can make a difference in the lives of other people. Teach me.*

Ask yourself:

- Where do I get caught up, stuck and fail to move forward because I am waiting for everything to be perfect?
- What has God shown me or spoken to me about His plan for my life and future, even if it didn't make sense at the time?
- Am I willing to use what God has placed in me for His purposes?

Affirmations:

I am called according to God's purposes.
God qualifies me and does not require perfection.
I boldly shine my inner light and express my true radiance.

2.
Stop Hiding – It's Your Time to Shine

Are you hiding from your place? Some of us know what our place is (or at least have some clues about it), yet we remain in hiding.

One Sunday morning, my pastor said, *"On the other side of your obedience, there are people waiting."* In other words, be obedient to the call God has for your life. People are waiting to be influenced by you, inspired by you, taught by you, helped by you, loved by you. That is thought-provoking truth for each of us to realize.

> "On the other side of your obedience, there are people waiting."

You were created by God to do a good work with greatness and impact. However, I am going to challenge you with this concept, which people who are spiritually maturing learn along the way:

What God has gifted you with, isn't about you. It's about His purposes, and you have a unique role to play within those purposes. Your gifts are for other people.

God has placed a unique set of characteristics, interests, gifts, and abilities in you. As we see in Ephesians 2:10, He has a special, good work for you to do, every day. What you have to offer will positively impact the world (the people) around you. I had to learn this lesson!

"So what's in it for me," some may wonder. Hold on to that thought. First, there is a maturity process that God works in each of us; in each of His people. If you look closely, this process is at work in our overall spiritual walk. As new believers, we are all about, "what can the Lord do for me." At some point, we move to becoming bond-servants. Part of conforming to the image of Christ is by becoming the willing hands and feet of the Lord.

They key word there is *willing*. You have a choice – to discover your God-given calling or not.

- Yes, you have the power of choice, whether to use your gifts or not, or to seek out His calling.

- Yes, being in God's calling for your life will bring your own soul deep satisfaction.
- Yes, you can even make a good living by using your gifts well.

Do not be mistaken and think there's no benefit for you. It is for you *and* for others at the same time. Knowing God's calling for you and stepping out to take that place invites God's power to work in your life. Do you want that?

Using and sharing your gifts will make you feel vitalized and more alive than you ever could be doing anything else. Do you want that?

Understanding who He has made you to be makes setting priorities, making decisions, choosing careers, planning, and selecting commitments much easier in life. Do you want that?

Knowing that you are in His will, on the right path for your life brings confidence, peace and trust that cannot be attained anywhere else. Do you want that?

I suspect you do. The point is it's not *all* about you. Who you are is about being a unique instrument in God's hand. Settling in to that ordained place makes all the difference in your own life's level of satisfaction, as well as making a difference in those around you. You've been blessed to be a blessing! Let God fill you up, so that you can then turn and pour out blessing on to others. This very much applies to your calling and gifts too!

Everything God has blessed you with (such as finances, talent, position, intelligence, authority, power, opportunity, etc.) isn't just for your own benefit either. God blesses you because He loves you, but also so that He can have a vessel to bless others through. Allow God to work *through* your life; receive, then pour out. Use what you've been given for furthering God's purposes.

> *"Praise be to the God and Father of our Lord Jesus Christ,*
> *who has blessed us in the heavenly realms with every*
> *spiritual blessing in Christ."* – Ephesians 1:3 (NIV)

Knowing your God-given gifts and His calling for you will touch all areas of your life, including things like;

- how to spend your time wisely,
- organizations to align yourself with,
- which relationships to build or sever,
- starting a business or ministry,
- what kind of education, training and learning opportunities to pursue,
- what to put focused energy into and what not to,
- career choices and work decisions, and
- how to best serve your community and church.

No matter what age you are, you can still realize your dreams!

Why is the Body Weak?

> *"...to prepare God's people for works of service, so that the body of Christ may be built up..."* – Ephesians 4:12 (NIV)

Remember the vision I shared about the body of Christ being weak? Why *is* the body of Christ weak right now?

There could be many possible answers to that question. A few reasons for this weakness might be a lack of biblical knowledge, no personal relationship with the Father, continuing to live in worldly ways, not using His full armor that is available, conforming to the image of our denomination, rather than to Jesus Himself, doubt and unbelief, compromise, idleness, giving in to fears, strongholds of sin, etc.

I also believe that *when God's people don't understand their own God-given calling, it seriously affects the body of Christ's effectiveness as a whole.*

> When God's people don't understand their own God-given calling, it seriously affects the body of Christ's effectiveness as a whole.

> *"Where there is no vision, the people perish..."* – Proverbs 29:18a (KJV)

We have each been born with unique natural abilities, talents, interests, and gifts which are used for a calling or purpose - God's purpose. You are here to further God's purposes on the earth. Whatever "it" is, God gave it to you, and it's not to be hidden any more. Jesus calls us the salt of the Earth and the light of the world. We have God's light of love to shine forth from within us. One way that you share that love and light is through using your unique set of gifts.

> *"You are the light of the world. A city on a hill cannot be hidden. Neither do people light a lamp and put it under a bowl. Instead they put it on its stand, and it gives light to everyone in the house. In the same way, let your light shine before men, that they may see your good deeds and praise your Father in heaven."* – Matthew 5:14-16 (NIV)

No more hiding your light or holding back your remarkable coolness! We know you are fearfully and wonderfully made. We are all in this time and place together. There is a sense of duty when it comes to discovering and taking our places. Your distinctive contribution is essential.

> *"Just as each of us has one body with many members, and these members do not all have the same function, so in Christ we who are many form one body, and each member belongs to all the others. We have different gifts, according to the grace given us."* – Romans 12:4-6a (NIV)

Have you ever thought about why God calls His people "the body" instead of referring to us as a group, community, congregation, or team? The concept of a body, a physical body, goes way beyond group, congregation or even what a team represents. Within a physical body there is no division, no lone ranger and no individual agendas. A body functions with many types of parts working in perfect unity, all going in the same direction. Every part is connected in coordinated motion.

Think about this: if we are members in the body of Christ, and Jesus is the head, how can we accomplish our specific calling if we do not share the thought process of our head? We need the mind of Christ to effectively take our place in the body of Christ. The head moves and directs the body.

- Can your feet move without being controlled by your head/mind?
- Can we as a body of believers move in the right direction without the head leading us?
- Can we as individuals know the will of the Father without having the mind of Christ?

Do you know your place or role? If the hand hasn't figured out it's a hand yet, it can't reach out effectively. Or if the foot has decided to retire its function, the rest of the body hobbles.

In the American Culture, we sometimes forget importance of having one role in the vast scheme of someone else's plan. The focus is on our individuality, which is unique and fun. But as believers in Christ, let us not set aside our co-dependency (in a positive way) on each other. Our diversity and different gifts are what make us more effective as a whole.

However, in the American church culture, I see an equally forgetful issue happening. Who you are and God's calling for you is not just about what you do on Sunday morning.

All day, every day, your gifts, talents and heart's desires are with you. I'm not sure about you, but the idea of being a person of faith only on Sunday mornings is not enough, and neither is using my God-given gifts and talents only once a week. Who we each are, is meant to be a 24/7 objective. *Purpose is alive, relentlessly.*

> Purpose
> is alive,
> relentlessly.

You were made for more! When you align yourself with God's calling for your whole life, you feel truly alive. When you can express your gifts in a meaningful way to those around you every day, your spirit soars.

My friend, women's pastor Danielle Payment, would say, "No matter what season of life you are in right now, hold on to your purpose." So no more hiding, okay? There are people waiting for you to use your gifts and know your calling. They need to be blessed by your blessings! God has plans, and your name is on the contributors list.

> *"Angels are very busy, so God calls regular people to step out and help with His miracles." –* Krista Dunk

Summary

As we spiritually mature, we move from an "us" focus, to an "others" focus. This is true even with our own gifts. Your gift is not for you; it is for the benefit of others, according to God's purposes. However, using your gifts and operating in His calling will benefit and satisfy your own soul like nothing other.

The body of Christ may be weakened because of His people not knowing their role, or place. One way that you share God's love with others is by expressing your gifts.

Jesus is the head of the church. We, collectively, are His body. To understand where the head is leading us, we need to hear from the Lord and become more Christ-like. When God's people remain unaware of their gifts and calling, it negatively affects the body of Christ's strength as a whole. Please don't hide your gifts, as your unique contribution is vital.

God's purposes are alive relentlessly. He has given you gifts to be used every day, not just on Sunday mornings.

Prayer: *Holy Lord, the only wise God, thank You for Your faithfulness and love. I want to know You more and be guided by You. Bless me so I can be a blessing to others. Your people, who are called by Your name, need strength. I need strength Lord. We humbly ask for Your wisdom.*

Ask yourself:

- Do I feel like I have purpose during this season of my life?
- Do I appreciate others with diverse gifts, or would I prefer everyone were more like me?
- Am I willing to be the hands and feet of the Lord, in whatever way He calls me?

Affirmations:

God has blessed me in the heavenly realms with every spiritual blessing in Christ.
I am blessed to be a blessing.
I joyfully play an important part in the body of Christ.
My purpose is alive, relentlessly.

I'm excited for you to discover what your special place is! Let's keep going...

3.
Find Joy Within Your Calling

"The expression of your gift is an act of worship to God." – Krista Dunk

Does this story sound familiar to you?

Katie and John are in their thirties and have been married for seven years. Katie grew up in church, and John started attending with Katie six years ago. Both serve in volunteer roles in their local church, which they are members of. Every-other weekend, John helps the usher team and also helps to organize the services. Katie volunteers her time editing videos of event footage and creating announcements for upcoming events.

They have several financial debts, including a mortgage for a home, two car payments and a line of credit. They feel stuck in their careers because of their financial commitments, and don't enjoy their work. Katie is a retail assistant manager and John works for their city's road maintenance department. Their jobs are secure and stable, but the jobs are not satisfying work. The problem is, they don't know what else to do and don't see any other options. In theory, they understand that God has a special purpose and plan for each person on the planet, but are unaware of what that plan would be for them.

Katie feels happy for her sister, Anna, who loves her preschool teaching job. Katie always knew Anna would eventually be working with young kids. She's always been good at that. Kids love her! But unfortunately, Katie has a growing frustration with the way her own life is going; knowing there has to be more that God has for her. She just doesn't feel like she is making a difference.

John doesn't think about it too much. The "daily grind," as he calls it, gives him a paycheck. However, his mind is constantly elsewhere, thinking about inventing. In his spare time he tinkers with projects, writes down ideas, and repeatedly fixes Mrs. Henderson's (the elderly next door neighbor) lawn mowers, small appliances and dryer when they malfunction. He has a shop full of projects and mechanical inventions.

Deep inside, each of them feels a sense of unsettled emptiness and longing to be used by God. Last Sunday's sermon on "God's Purposes" brought up more frustration for Katie. "If God has given me gifts and purpose, why don't I know what they are? I see the possibilities for others, but for me, all of this seems very unclear."

Dried Up Spirits

Katie and John's experience is very common. They have gifts, but are either unaware of them, or are unaware of what purpose they're for. They are caught up in working for money to pay bills and commitments, but find no passion or soul satisfaction in it. Don't get me wrong, it's great to have money and we all need some, but that is not the point. The real problem is that *inside, they feel like their spirits are slowly drying up.* Their lives are moving by quickly. Katie and John feel more like out-of-control observers of the outcome, than like owners of their own lives. I will be coming back to Katie and John's story later.

> Inside, they feel like their spirits are slowly drying up.

This is where many people "live" when it comes to gifts, talents, calling, and purpose. Sadly, this couple's experience is so common. I say "sadly" with sympathy, because it was very similar to the way my own life used to be. I can talk about this with complete conviction, being conscious of how sad and frustrating it was to be in that place of dryness and dissatisfaction!

Here is what my own personal experience was like:

Growing up, I developed a very practical mind and way of thinking that was focused on stability, security and mediocre status-quo. I knew I had many talents, gifts and abilities, but somehow those were not important in the realm of creating a life and career.

My first "real job" was at a real estate office, where I was a secretary and accounts payable bookkeeper. It was a good job and fairly interesting, but living in Olympia, the capital city of Washington State, the goal for many people in my community is to get a state job. About one year later, it happened - I got my first state job! It was so exciting...except for the fact that the job itself was mind-numbingly horrible.

Truly, it was a daily grind of nothing but data entry into a computer. I did it well and was a well-respected worker, but since this job offered zero creativity, it was tedious, dreary work for me. Outside of my work hours, I went from one idea to the next, from project to project, trying to satisfy my need for a creative outlet and entrepreneurial adventure.

I moved up in job classifications through the seven years I worked for the state. I ended up working for a division chief, where the opportunity for some creative thought existed. Even so, this new state office job still felt like an empty box to me. Cubicle jail! I knew there had to be more. "Please God, there has to be more!"

At this job, God made it clear to me that I was to learn sign language. So, I went back to college to study at an interpreter training program. Learning sign language was easy for me and it felt like a natural fit.

When an interpreting job was offered to me from a local high school, I was torn. The pay was less than what I was making, the work hours were less, and I honestly wasn't sure my skills were ready. On paper, going to work for the high school made no practical sense at all. However, I prayerfully made the decision to take it and was later thankful that I did!

About a year later, my son was born and I became a stay-home mom. Having me stay home once we had children had been the goal for our family. Although I was (and still am) thankful for that opportunity, I slowly began to feel bland, discontented and frustrated, and then guilty about having those feelings too. I knew God has dreams for His people, and I wanted to know what His dreams were for me. My quest to find answers began with these simultaneous feelings of discontentment and reflection.

During this time, my husband and I found a new church home where we were challenged to grow spiritually, personally and in leadership ability. I can honestly say it was the first place in my life that had challenged my thinking and mindsets. And then one day I had the thought, "What is my personal potential, anyway? If I develop myself and figure out what God has for me, what could I accomplish?"

> "What is my personal potential, anyway? If I develop myself and figure out what God has for me, what could I accomplish?"

That was a life-changing question that still motivates me inside today. My mission now is to use everything God has given me, and to leave nothing behind. I found this quote, which fits my intentions perfectly:

*"When I stand before God at the end of my life I would hope
that I would have not a single bit of talent left and could say,
'I used everything You gave me.'"* -Erma Bombeck

Since then, I've intentionally challenged myself to grow and get out of my "little box" mentality and easy comfort zone. Discovering, embracing, developing, and using my God-given gifts have been part of my transformation. The process has been invigorating, difficult, humbling, compelling, stressful, rewarding, tiring, and exciting all at the same time!

I believe God has placed a deep need for purpose within us. Maybe you, or someone you know, have had thoughts like these at some point in life:

- Why am I here?
- What is my purpose?
- Why do other people have joy and satisfaction in what they do, and I don't?
- Am I making a difference?
- Isn't there something more?
- God, what is your plan for my life and what special gifts do I have?

I have to say, the question, "What is my purpose?" needs a slight adjustment. I believe my purpose is to know God, and to avail myself to Him as a unique instrument He can use. Ultimately, it's not about *my* purpose or *your* purpose, but God's purposes. Within His purposes however, we do have a role or mission specific to us. God definitely created you with purpose in mind. "Who am I within God's purposes?" is a more accurate question.

Some people aren't self-aware enough to consciously ask these questions, but may experience a mid-life crisis or depression because the root of this deep need for purpose remains unsatisfied.

Spirit of Competition

There's another potential issue when we don't know our gifts and calling: Coveting and an unhealthy spirit of competition can spring up within us. For example, let's say you know someone who is operating in their calling and gifting. When you observe them, it is easy to covet their gifts and feel frustrated. "If she can do that, I want to be able to do that too," or "he speaks with authority and why do I not get that opportunity?"

If you or I say, "I want their gift," the reality is that their gift is not what we need. What we need is to discover *our own* calling - *our* role - *our* gifts. We need to know what we've got, and then we can settle in and feel satisfied.

On the flip side, when we know our role, when we know our calling, supporting, celebrating and rallying for others who are within their gifting comes more easily. When you're confident in what God has for you, you can then celebrate what God has for others. A competitive spirit melts away and collaboration, encouragement and a heart open to receive from that person's gift takes its place.

When we are confident in our own gifts and calling, we can be a better support for, and celebrate, someone else when they're operating in theirs. Then, by example, you encourage others to step out and take their places too.

There is joy within your calling; joy for you, joy for others and joy for God. Your calling represents a win-win-win situation! Joy and significance will replace the dryness and mundane existence.

> When we are confident in our own gifts and calling, we can be a better support for, and celebrate, someone else when they're operating in theirs.

Next, let's discuss The Gift Discovery Cycle™ and begin an important step towards stepping out to take your place – gift discovery.

Summary

Many people are unsatisfied with their jobs, careers and businesses. They're unaware of their gifts and do not have a vision for God's calling for them. It may cause them to feel dry inside. Many people are simply working for money and do not find the significance that their souls long for.

Have you ever asked yourself, "What is my personal potential?" At the end of your life, I pray that you will be able to look back and know you used everything God gave you. Avail yourself to God and His purposes, rather than working your plan and purposes.

Be aware of an unhealthy spirit of competition that can spring up when it comes to gifts and callings. Knowing your own call and role helps you support and celebrate what God has for other people, rather competing.

When you express your gifts and operate in your calling, God wins, you win and those whose lives you are meant to impact win!

Prayer: *Father, in You there is fullness of joy. Great and mighty is Your name! Fill me with Your joy. I don't want any more feelings of dryness in my soul and spirit. Help my heart and mind not compare myself with others, or to ever feel insignificant or inferior. I am Your creation; Your child. You have made everything glorious, including me. Thank You for the work You are doing in me.*

Ask yourself:

- If God is with me, what *is* my personal potential?
- Do I celebrate others' gifts, or do I covet or compete with them?
- When have I traded my dreams for security? Is it possible to have both?

Affirmations:

I am used by God for good work.
I use everything God has given me for His purposes.
Because of my example, others are encouraged to step out and take their places too.
When I use my gifts, there is abundant joy.

Get ready for The Gift Discovery Cycle™…

4.
The Gift Discovery Cycle™

The Gift Discovery Cycle™:

Frustration – Desire – Seeking –
Awareness – Development – Renew –
Share – Give Back – Maintenance

The Gift Discovery Cycle™ is the process, or flow, that I have observed in my life. It visually illustrates the journey of discovering gifts, developing them, growing personally and spiritually, and then operating in them on a regular basis. It's a strategy, a road map per say to get you from where you are now to where you want to be with understanding and using your gifts. More importantly than where *you* want to be; where *God* wants you to be.

I cannot personally tell you what your gifts are, but I know who can. God holds the keys to that knowledge, and He desires for you to have it.

"He who has begun a good work in you will complete it until the day of Jesus Christ." – Philippians 1:6 (NKJV)

By observing The Gift Discovery Cycle™ happening in your own life, you'll know the phase you are currently in and what you need to be learning and working on. During each phase, you can connect with God, asking Him for His wisdom and plan, and anticipate what is coming next.

If you wonder why I've named this a cycle instead of a process, here is my explanation; although it would be great to run through each step once and be done forever, calling it good for the rest of your life, instead it is more like painting a house.

Painting a house is a process that goes from scraping, taping, priming, and spraying, to trimming, clean-up, and touch-up. For a while afterward, it seems completed and just needs a bit of maintenance now and then. After several years, the phases will no doubt need to be revisited again!

Rarely, if ever, does God approve of stagnation. Jabez prayed, *"Oh, that you would bless me and enlarge my territory! Let your hand be with me…"* It was a prayer that aligned with God's will, and God granted it. He loves to do a new thing, and He will grow you again as your personal capacity and stewardship increases.

Let's take a quick look at each step along the cycle. When you look at each of these phases, you can probably identify which one you're in right now. Looking back, you will recognize phases you've already experienced. It is possible to be in more than one phase simultaneously.

Frustration

This stage of the cycle probably needs no in-depth explanation. It's when you feel frustrated! Maybe you see others who have clear purpose and vision for what God has for them and it makes you mad that you don't. Let's be honest – sometimes it takes someone else who has something that we don't to motivate us to get our rears in gear. Or, maybe you're simply a new believer trying to figure this all out. Or, maybe you feel frustrated about how your life has turned out. Or, you have heard the message that

God has a plan for your life, yet you have no idea what that plan is. Or, it might be that you feel like your life has lost purpose.

In any case, thankfully you don't need to remain in this frustrated phase any longer. Whether it stemmed from noticing someone else operating in their gifts, from an inner dissatisfaction with the way your life is going or some other event, being aware of your dissatisfaction is a good thing. If you realize your frustration stems from not knowing what your calling is, then congratulations! It is a step in the right direction.

Awareness of why you're frustrated gives you the power to do something about it and move forward. The only reason we pursue change is when we are no longer willing to accept "less than."

Certified counselor and former pastor, Dr. Rick Miller, has worked with hundreds of people working through hurts and looking for purpose. When I asked him about what he's noticed when God's people don't know His calling for them, he had this observation; *"I find this is the case with almost every believer. They do not know what God's calling for their life is, and it causes them to flounder in their Christian life."*

During our conversation, he also made this observation, *"Many of us think that God's will is super-specific. It's not like asking a child, 'what do you want to be when you grow up?', but more like 'do you want to become like Him when you grow up?'"* He added that we should be asking ourselves *who* we want to be when we grow up, emphasizing our character qualities and service rather than some specific position.

You may be in the frustrated phase if any or all of these apply to you:

- You feel inside that God has more for you, but aren't sure what it is.
- Life seems dull, routine and purpose seems missing.
- You are unaware of what your gifts and/or calling are.
- You want more out of life.
- It irritates you or makes you envious when other people are freely operating in their calling.
- Life isn't working well so far, and you are not sure why.

Desire

If you choose to move out of frustration, desire comes next. *Desire happens when you are no longer content to go with life's default flow.* You're ready to know what God has for you. Desire is what happens when you realize something is missing, and you're ready to take the next step forward to get wisdom.

> Desire happens when you are no longer content to go with life's default flow.

The desire to discover what more is out there can be urgent, or even tentative. Your behavior in the desire phase shows a lot about your self-esteem, drive, confidence, level of commitment towards growth, and personality. If you feel apprehensive about moving forward, take a careful look at why you feel that way. It *is* God's will for you to get this wisdom. Is your desire to know your gifts and calling greater than your hesitations?

You may be in the desire phase if you can relate to any or all of these:

- When you bought this book, you knew this topic is what you needed to learn more about.
- You understand that the reason why you've been frustrated about life is related to not yet knowing your God-given gifts or calling.
- You say to yourself, "I have got to figure this thing out!"
- You feel the deep longing to understand and move forward, but are not sure what exactly to do next.
- You often pray and ask God about discovering His calling on your life, but are not sure what else you can do.
- Messages and sermons on gifts, purpose and calling inspire you, and you know now is the time to take action.

Seeking

The seeking phase is where you're taking action to get wisdom. During this time period, you're on the hunt for wisdom, resources, deep in prayer, at a place of inquiry in many areas of your life. It is time to seek God, asking Him first about the gifts He has given you, then about the bigger picture of your life's calling. Through the Holy Spirit, God will teach you hidden things when you ask and seek with all your heart. Elements of action in the seeking phase include asking, collecting knowledge, praying, listening, persistence, and being intentional.

Seeking has two important components – seeking in the spiritual realm, and also the practical, natural steps. Both are very important for your journey. Many ideas and methods for effective seeking (in both realms) are discussed in the Discovery Section of this book.

You may be in the seeking phase if:

- You scour the Bible and study this topic.
- You enroll in workshops, Bible studies and/or classes that teach on life purpose, spiritual gifts, etc.
- Resources on this topic found on the web or in bookstores always catch your attention.
- People notice there is something different about you lately.
- God is showing you new things about yourself that you never noticed before, or is bringing long-forgotten memories up.
- You're fasting and praying regularly and persistently seeking God for His will for your life.

Awareness

Awareness is an exciting phase that blossoms like an extravagant flower; sometimes twisting and peeking open slowly, other times bursting suddenly open all at once. This is when you start to get clarity and clues, to "see" and become aware of your special God-given gifts and calling.

Gifts are revealed in this phase, and with this new revelation, a person can choose to embrace their gifts or to shun them. Sometimes, we realize we've been shutting them out for years! Talking to myself right now... And other times we realize they've been right in front of our faces, yet just couldn't see them.

Speaking of embracing vs. rejecting our gifts, let me use Tinkerbell as an example. For those of you with preschool daughters, granddaughters, nieces, or neighbors, you probably know these little ladies love Tinkerbell. She has a great story about learning to embrace her gift.

If you don't already know, Tinkerbell is a fairy. Her world is a community of fairies; segregated by their type of gifting. Each has a very specific gift and duty. There are water fairies, singing and musical fairies, tinker fairies, garden fairies, animal fairies, pixie dust fairies, etc.

For a long time, Tinkerbell rejected her "tinker" (builder) gift. She longed to have one of the more glamorous gifts, like the water or garden fairies did. She tried and tried to take on these other gifts, but to no avail. Her gift wasn't valuable in her own eyes. In the eyes of the other fairies, she was *so* good at what she did, but in her own eyes, it came so easily that it was nothing of value to her (and it was boring).

I learned these two lessons from Tinkerbell about gifts:

1. Sometimes we try to shun our own gifts.
2. Sometimes we try to fit ourselves into a gift that doesn't fit.

It's sort of like that pair of shoes I bought on clearance last year. They were such a great deal…The only problem was they were a half size too small. Maybe you have a pair like this too.

Every time I wear them, I regret it. They just don't fit well, but I really want them to fit! They're cute, stylish and were a cheap deal. Unfortunately, they do not suit me. They are someone else's size. I'm forcing myself into something that doesn't fit.

You can want someone else's gift. You can shun your own. You can try and try to force yourself into a shoe that doesn't fit, or you can embrace and develop what you have. When you operate within your gifting, that is when you shine. It might not be flashy or trendy, but it is a perfect match with the essence of you. Not only that, but it also fills an important need in the lives of others.

Anyway, back to the awareness phase. This is the time period when you're becoming more aware of what God has for your life and work. Words such as; clues, ah-ha, vision, revelation, knowledge, correlation, and insight help describe this phase. There is a real sense of freedom that comes with becoming aware of what God has placed in you.

You may be in the awareness phase if any or all of these apply to you:

- You know what your unique gifts are.
- God has revealed new things to you that seem to bring puzzle pieces of your life together.
- You have new vision about the future God has for you.
- You have a clear next step in front of you.

- The new awareness you have makes you feel exhilarated and excited.
- The new awareness you have makes you feel a bit nervous or unworthy.

Development

Now that you're aware of your gifts and may have some clues about your calling, it is time to start developing your gifts, getting wisdom, finding appropriate training and education, etc. Be aware that while in this phase, you may not necessarily have the big picture yet, but possibly just knowledge of the next step or direction. That's okay!

Really, we grow continuously with our gifts as we mature spiritually, but it's at this step that we launch out to start purposefully developing them. As we go through our lives, aware of God's calling, we are continually being refined and strengthened for our work. Our gifts and personal capacity are molded as we grow into effective stewards.

Unfortunately, this phase can be a stopping place for many people. Do not let that be you. To become aware of your gifts is awesome, although ultimately unhelpful if you stop your forward progress there. Move forward with development, where you learn and hone your gifts. When your gifts are fully developed, that is when they'll be most effective to impact the world in a positive way as a part of your overall calling.

In the Growth Section of this book, we'll be discussing many options and ideas on how to develop your gifts to their fullest to have maximum impact in the world.

You may be in the development phase if:

- You are being discipled or mentored by someone.
- Furthering your education is taking a significant amount of your time right now.
- You feel driven to learn everything you can about a specific topic.
- Right now, you are working on skill building through classes, workshops, training, etc.
- Your personal capacity and knowledge are increasing.
- You've been practicing with your gifts.
- You realize you have a lot to learn.

As a part of the development and renew phases, be a student of wisdom; meaning stay open to improvement, learning opportunities, growth, and correction. Sometimes our pride can keep us from being teachable, so be vigilant to remain teachable. *Trustworthy sources and mentors, who have your best interests in mind, are strategic relationships God places along your life's journey.* Stay open to learning from people who are friends to your destiny.

> *"Be a friend to the destinies of others."* – Pastor Dave Minton

> Trustworthy sources and mentors, who have your best interests in mind, are strategic relationships God places along your life's journey.

Renew

In the renew phase, personal growth is happening in a spiritual way. The biggest part of the renew phase is the renewing of your mind. God has plans for your life, but if your mindset is stuck on the old you, the new you can never step out to take your rightful place. In fact, *the "new you" starts in your mind and heart through the information God gives you.*

> The "new you" starts in your mind and heart through the information God gives you.

The renewal phase can be tough, but ultra-rewarding for those willing to do the work it requires. This is the phase where you'll need to deal with your "stuff," such as insecurities, baggage from the past, issues, pride, selfishness, doubts, and self-esteem. It's also the time when you can redefine what is possible in your life.

What is inside our hearts and minds eventually makes its way to the surface, showing up in our attitudes, actions and words. The renew phase is about changing what's inside first, to affect change on what flows out of us. As you can imagine, this has everything to do with being good stewards of our calling and gifts.

Quite honestly, I'm not sure this phase is ever quite complete! No matter how long we've been on a discovery journey with the Lord, there is always more work to be done in this area of renewal. Like I said though, it's hard, yet extremely rewarding. Are you willing to do the hard work of renewal?

You may be in the renew phase if any or all of these apply to you:

- You are re-evaluating priorities and commitments in your life.
- Setting new goals is on your mind lately.
- You've realized that your own mindset and limiting beliefs have been holding you back.
- You are actively getting wisdom about renewing your mind.
- Who you see yourself as is changing, bit by bit, to conform to who God sees you as.
- Your issues and "stuff" are coming up, and it feels uncomfortable, yet eye-opening.
- God is speaking to you about who you are – the "being" not just what you do.

Share

Yep. It's that time - time to share your gifts and to officially *Step Out and Take Your Place!* Are you ready? You will usually think you aren't, or at least that is how it's been for me. God has called me to step out into His calling for me, piece by piece, and so far I haven't felt qualified or ready to take the step at the time when the door of opportunities opened.

Chances are you won't be completely finished developing your gifts or renewing your mindset yet during this take-action phase. You'll think to yourself, "but I have so much more still to learn!" It's true that using your gifts can be like on-the-job training at times!

Yes, sharing can be a scary step, but exciting too. As my bold sister, Trisha, would say, "do something that scares you every day." Good advice from someone who has taken a lot of action, and understands how to put herself "out there."

Start out small if you need to. Do not despise small beginnings. Instead, practice sharing your gifts whenever possible. When opportunities matching your interests, gifts and calling arise at church, work or in other settings, go for it. Doing this will help you gain confidence. By doing this, it will also help confirm God's will for your life.

For a moment, let's go back to the point about small beginnings. The Bible specifically tells us to not despise small beginnings. Why? Because we tend to!

If you are like me, and have a vision for the big picture calling (that you know is coming sometime in the future), despising the smallness you are experiencing right now is tempting. When I have felt that way, I need to stop, take a deep breath, and know that God has me right here, right now, learning and experiencing everything I need to learn here, now. Then, I can be ready to do a great job at the next level.

Honestly, we'd probably fail and then be discouraged if we jumped right into the big vision without going through the small beginnings steps. The "small beginnings" time period is our training ground and builds confidence and trust in God.

> *"Though your beginning was insignificant, yet your end will increase greatly."* – Job 8:7 (NASB)

For example, let's say I am used to speaking in front of audiences of 100 or less for 30-45 minutes and running three hour workshops for 25 people. Tomorrow, can I jump in to the vision I have for running full weekend retreats or speaking on TV? I could try to jump from level one to level ten in one leap, although it might not be pretty. In fact, I might bomb and get very discouraged.

God will grow us, step-by-step, to the level of His vision for us. Along the way, He will also connect us up with those who teach us, partner up and collaborate with us (and we with them), as a part of their calling. There are other people who are part of your journey.

By the way, did you know that "your place" grows and evolves? Yes. Another good reason for calling this a cycle! The example above helps to demonstrate that journey of growth and evolution. Using my example, notice that my overall calling remains the same (teaching and encouraging God's people, in the area of expression, gifts and calling), although the capacity, wisdom, environment, recipients, and scale in which it is accomplished continues to grow and morph.

You may be in the sharing phase if any or all of these apply to you:

- You don't feel completely ready or qualified yet, but opportunities and doors are opening for you to share your gifts.
- You've seized the opportunities to share your gifts with others; the opportunities that you know are leading you towards your calling.

- People (bosses, pastors, friends, etc.) are starting to notice your strengths and gifts, and call on you to use them.
- It is easier now to make decisions about which teams, committees, projects, and other opportunities to accept or decline.
- There is a new freedom of expression that you feel because of sharing your gifts with others.
- There is a new sense of purpose inside.
- You understand how your gifts fit into your overall calling, and are walking that path.

Give Back

The ultimate "it's not about me" phase, giving back brings you full circle. The give back phase has two parts to it:

1. Using your gifts and what you have learned to contribute to the lives of others.
2. Giving glory and honor to God, to Whom it is due.

Giving back can mean using time, money, resources, or knowledge to give others a hand up. It is also time to help other people who have similar gifts as you do, or a similar calling, to reach their full potential.

During this time, you could become a mentor, coach, teacher, writer, spiritual mother or father, or other type of leader who demonstrates God's power being available to others. If you are a business owner for example, your business or company (or personal finances) could go above and beyond tithing to support Kingdom causes or non-profit work.

There is high value in sharing what you've learned and experienced. Your testimony of discovering, developing and sharing your gifts and finding God's calling in your life gives others hope, inspires them and strengthens their faith. Your testimony could be the catalyst for someone else to step out and take their place.

Speaking of hope, be mindful of remaining authentic and honest about your imperfections. When others see how powerfully God has used you, it will help them understand that God is more than enough. By doing so, you give others hope that He can use anyone who is willing and who's heart is dedicated and open to Him, despite their imperfections.

Secondly, it is essential that you continue to acknowledge God, and He will continue to direct your path. The more you dive into using your God-given gifts and know your everyday calling, the more you realize you cannot do this work in your own power. If you could do this work in your own strength, it wouldn't be a calling from God.

God, the Giver of gifts deserves all the praise! This phase has a weakness to it, but that is its' strength as well. Keep your heart on His altar, and practice thankfulness.

> *"So I commend the enjoyment of life, because nothing is better for*
> *a man under the sun than to eat and drink and be glad. Then*
> *joy will accompany him in his work all the days of the life God*
> *has given him under the sun."* – Ecclesiastes 8:15 (NIV)

You personally get soul satisfaction from using what God has given you, right? Right, so you and I will be wise to remember that we are nothing, or can do nothing of value, without the Lord. Do not fall into the mindset that you are self-sufficient. Instead, always honor and rely on the All-Sufficient One. Give back to Him, with your tithes, prayers, praise, worship, faith, love, service, and heart!

You may be in the give back phase if:

- People ask you to teach them what you know.
- You're sharing the testimony of your personal calling journey with others.
- You're in a place where you are able to give back, either financially, with your time and energy, wisdom, and/or service.
- Others say you are inspiring them to discover their gifts and God's calling for their own life.
- You've become a more willing and obedient person that God can use. When He speaks, you listen and act more often than before.

Maintenance

When you've reached the maintenance phase, your current level of personal capacity and how you're operating in your calling becomes normal to you. At this time, you're using your gifts on a regular basis. Yes, it may still be challenging for your schedule and energy level at times, but it is no longer challenging your skills. You are able to maintain doing the work God has for you at this level with a sense of ease.

Maintenance is not a negative phase to be in, but if you are following God's lead, He will move you out of it. Trust me when I say that you have not "arrived." We do not reach a place (until we reach Heaven) where God says, "Okay Susie, you made it. This personal capacity, this level of operation, this location and same people to influence, this set of experiences, and this current understanding you have is exactly where I'd like you to stay for the rest of your life."

That's not going to happen.

The only thing I know for sure is that God will challenge your status quo. During periods of growth is when your faith is challenged and strengthened. God wants that for you. He also wants that for the people you are meant to influence.

So, do not be surprised if you find yourself meandering back into The Gift Discovery Cycle™ step 1 again; frustration. Be watchful for feelings of frustration or traces of dissatisfaction to crop up again. It just means it's time to grow again, and change is coming. That is a good thing! A new layer (or level) of your everyday calling may be on its way…

Evidence that you might be in the maintenance phase includes:

- You no longer feel challenged by your current level of operation.
- The decisions you make and actions you take seem to be more automatic, predictable, routine, and comfortable.
- You don't feel like you're learning anything new lately, or being challenged to grow.
- You feel in your spirit that God wants to do a new thing, and change is coming.
- When you can say to yourself, "I can do this," and find yourself praying less for God's assistance.

Note: Once you start down this road of discovery of higher purpose, I encourage you to keep moving forward. You'll notice that stopping the forward progress will nag at your mind and frustrate your spirit.

A word of caution for you during The Gift Discovery Cycle™ - Avoid the Ego Trap

Speaking of not having "arrived" yet, meaning we haven't become the ultimate master of...well...anything yet, really...

There are three potential traps, when it comes to our gifts that go hand-in-hand. They are;

1. Ego
2. Becoming unteachable, and
3. Seeking recognition and glory for self.

Each of these traps stem from a prideful attitude. I've been guilty of falling into all of these traps at one point or another, and they're a dangerous hindrance to destiny. They're also a hindrance for receiving God's grace and provision.

Recently, I read an attention-grabbing status update from a friend in one of my online social networks. They said that EGO stands for "Edging God Out."

Decide to be a student of wisdom; meaning stay open to improvement, learning opportunities, growth, and correction. It's all too easy to think we have "arrived," and then become stiff-necked and unteachable. This is where we must tear down our pride if we truly want to be sensitive to the work the Holy Spirit is doing through us (and in us).

During every phase of The Gift Discovery Cycle™, you'll have plenty of spiritual growth left to go. It is something to keep in mind every day from now on. Say this to yourself right now:

"Lord, with Your help, I am on my way!"

Summary

The Gift Discover Cycle™ is a visual depiction of the process of discovering, developing and sharing gifts. The cycle steps are:

1. Frustration
2. Desire
3. Seeking

4. Awareness
5. Development
6. Renew
7. Share
8. Give Back
9. Maintenance

By observing The Gift Discovery Cycle™ happening in your own life, you'll know the phase you are currently in and what you need to be learning and working on. During each phase, you can connect with God, asking Him for His wisdom and plan, and anticipate what is coming next. During every phase of The Gift Discovery Cycle™, you will have plenty of spiritual growth left to go.

Prayer: *Lord, my Rock and Redeemer, I know You have good plans for me. All Your ways are good, and all Your plans are sure. Keep me on the journey to discover who I am. I want to know You more and learn from You. What You have for me is amazing, so I pray that you continue to guide me to it. Thank You God.*

Ask yourself:

- Which phase(s) am I in now?
- Have I been forcing myself into things that don't fit me?
- Who are my mentors, and what am I learning from them?
- Do I keep an attitude that's open to learning, no matter what level I'm at in my spiritual growth?
- Will I choose to keep moving through phases of The Gift Discovery Cycle™, or stay stuck?

Affirmations:

I am gifted!
I eagerly practice sharing my gifts whenever possible.
The gifts God has given me are very valuable, and I cherish them.
I am a student of wisdom, and never stop learning and growing myself.

Discovery

5.
You, 101

Have you ever taken a class on the topic of…you? Welcome, class, to You, 101. God, the Creator of you, will be your instructor as we work through this course.

Okay, now I'm being slightly silly, but seriously, we have a lot to learn about who we are! Beyond knowing our God-given gifts, comes knowing the big picture - His calling for our life. Our gifts fit into our calling.

As a simple visual, here is the progressive lesson plan for discovering your life's calling (along with how they align with The Gift Discovery Cycle's™ steps):

1. **Learn who I am in Christ**
(Aligns with the "desire and seeking" phases)

⇩

2. **Know what my gifts are**
(Aligns with the "awareness" phase)

⇩

3. **See the calling God has for me**
(Part of the overall cycle from "awareness" on)

⇩

4. **Gain the confidence, skill and mindset to live it**
(Aligns with the "renew" phase)

⇩

5. **Allow the continuing, refining work of God to conform me into the image of Christ**
(Part of the overall cycle)

Each necessary lesson lays a foundation for the next.

Let's conquer the first tier of our lesson plan now – ***Learn who I am in Christ.***

In His life handbook (the Bible), God has promises for you as His chosen vessel. You can get this transformational truth by reading the Bible, listening to accurate biblical teaching and having the voice of the Lord speak something to you directly.

What does it mean to "know who I am in Christ?"
This phrase talks about having an inner understanding about God's knowledge of you vs. your knowledge of yourself (as you see yourself). He created you, and He has an eternal perspective of what true reality is. He knows every aspect of who you are, including every weakness and ability and what your full potential is. He also knows the dreams He has for you; a plan of how, where, when and why these aspects of you are meant to be used.

Knowing who you are in Christ also has to do with understanding God's promises. To each person who has faith in Him and who follows His commands, God gives them special privileges and promises. There are literally thousands of promises to us as His people (found in the Bible), and without the knowledge of what they are, we don't know what's rightfully ours. Also, when we don't know who we are in Christ, we see our limited resources, limited ability and our current situation as the only reality we can expect.

> *"And we know that God causes everything to work together for the good of those who love God and are called according to his purpose for them. For God knew his people in advance, and he chose them to become like his Son, so that his Son would be the firstborn among many brothers and sisters. And having chosen them, he called them*

to come to him. And having called them, he gave them right standing with himself. And having given them right standing, he gave them his glory. What shall we say about such wonderful things as these? If God is for us, who can ever be against us?" – Romans 8:28-31 (NLT)

These truths below are vital for you to learn, know and believe, as a part of knowing who you are in Christ:

- All who confess that Jesus is Lord become a new creation, and have access to God directly through Jesus
- God created you with special gifts and abilities
- You are called, according to His purposes
- God has a good future, full of hope, planned for you
- He will never leave you or forsake you
- You have been made more than a conqueror through Christ, meant to be victorious, despite hardships
- You have a vital role within His body of believers
- God uses regular people for extraordinary work, if they are willing
- Ask, and you will receive what is according to God's will
- Your calling has eternal significance

Did you notice how I used the phrase "learn, know and believe" these truths? Learning who you are in Christ starts with head knowledge (through reading and hearing), then moves to your heart as you start to understand and believe it. The information comes in, and then it takes root and grows.

Without this stable foundation of knowing who you are in Christ, you'll struggle during your search for purpose and calling. With this foundational information, you can continue to build on it, getting more wisdom about His plan for your life. His promises are sure!

Homework for this lesson: Read your Bible and meditate on who God says you are in Him. Read more about His promises for you as His child. Allow the head knowledge to settle in to your heart as a new reality and belief. Afterward, proclaim, *"I know who I am!"*

It's time to keep building with lesson plan section 2 - ***Know what my gifts are.***

"I know who I am!"

You are gifted. God is no respecter of persons (meaning He does not hold certain people in higher esteem) and He has freely given special gifts to each of us. Your unique gifts and abilities could include any number of things, such as musical gifts, high IQ, artistic ability, mechanical or technical gifts, physical coordination, leadership, administrative gifting, compassion, mathematical skill, spiritual discernment, or many other possibilities.

Your gift may not be some kind of Earth-shattering, brilliant ability, like memorizing an entire yellow pages directory, being a world-famous musical genius or leaping a tall building in a single bound. It might be regular, everyday things that you're really good at. I know that may not be glamorous or glitzy news, but every single, non-flashy gift is desperately needed too.

The calling God has for your life involves your gifts, so it's time to find out what you've got. As God's creation, you and I have many facets that make up who we are. It's time to do some investigation work and study yourself closely.

During the Discovery Section of this book, we'll be talking about a variety of ways in which you can study yourself, including things like:

- Taking personality tests
- Prayer and fasting
- Spiritual gifts assessments
- Seeking God for His revelation
- Journaling
- Evaluating your Calling Components™ (more in chapter 7)
- Continuing to study who you are in Christ
- Talking with mentors

These are just a few of the ideas we'll cover. Expect to learn more about these and others as we continue to move through the Discovery Section.

Just to be clear, this book will not tell you what your individual gifts are. It does provide you a valuable framework and strategy to use to gain that knowledge from God. With clear next steps, it becomes much easier to move forward.

As with anything valuable and significant to be gained in life, I can tell you that there's no magic pill or "easy button" method for gift discovery. If it were super easy, we'd all have the answer to that question, and I suspect the world would be a better place.

I can tell you though, that when you have an awareness of your gifts, where, how, why, and for whom to use them for, you've tapped into a source of power straight from God. You will see Him working in what you do, instead of feeling like it's all your own effort and ideas.

Homework for this lesson: See chapters 6 through 9 for gift discovery strategies.

<u>What comes next in You, 101?</u> ***See the calling God has for me.***

Once you know who you are in Christ, and know what your God-given gifts are, it's the perfect time to ask God about His calling for your life. Since we haven't gone in-depth yet on how to discover your gifts, I will skim this topic for now. Chapter 9 has all the information regarding seeking God about your overall calling. I do, however, have one quick thought to share with you now.

Through this discovery journey, you'll gain confidence through knowing that you are in God's will for your calling. Have you ever wondered, "Am I called to this, or is it of man? Am I working my own plan (or another person's) or God's plan here?" A great example of being "God appointed vs. an appointment by man" is the story of David and King Saul.

Clearly, the Bible shows that David was God's chosen man to be king of Israel. Saul, on the other hand, was the people's choice. As we read in 1 Samuel 8 (NLT), the elders of Israel met with Samuel the prophet, and this was their request:

"Give us a king to judge us like all the other nations have."

Samuel was displeased with their request and went to the LORD for guidance. "Do everything they say to you," the LORD replied, "for it is me they are rejecting, not you. They don't want me to be their king any longer. Ever since I brought them from Egypt they have continually abandoned me and followed other gods. And now they are giving you the same treatment. Do as they ask, but solemnly warn them about the way a king will reign over them."

So Samuel passed on the LORD's warning to the people who were asking him for a king. "This is how a king will reign over you," Samuel said. "The king will draft your sons..." (verses 11b-18 has a long list of hardships the king will impose on the people)

But the people refused to listen to Samuel's warning. "Even so, we still want a king," they said. "We want to be like the nations around us. Our king will judge us and lead us into battle."

So Samuel repeated to the Lord *what the people had said, and the* Lord *replied, "Do as they say, and give them a king." Then Samuel agreed and sent the people home." (verses 5a-22)*

Saul become their king, and saw some success for a season. I am going to pick up the story again in chapter 15, where Samuel tells King Saul;

"Since you have rejected the Lord's *command, he has rejected you as king of Israel."*

As Samuel turned to go, Saul tried to hold him back and tore the hem of his robe. And Samuel said to him, "The Lord *has torn the kingdom of Israel from you today and has given it to someone else—one who is better than you. And he who is the Glory of Israel will not lie, nor will he change his mind, for he is not human that he should change his mind!" (verses 26b-29)*

Now the Lord *said to Samuel, "You have mourned long enough for Saul. I have rejected him as king of Israel, so fill your flask with olive oil and go to Bethlehem. Find a man named Jesse who lives there, for I have selected one of his sons to be my king." (verse 16:1)*

When Samuel arrives, he sees that Jesse has many sons. The eldest son stepped forward and Samuel thought, *"Surely this is the* Lord's *anointed!"*

But the Lord *said to Samuel, "Don't judge by his appearance or height, for I have rejected him. The* Lord *doesn't see things the way you see them. People judge by outward appearance, but the* Lord *looks at the heart." (verses 16:6-7)*

The Lord continued to reject all of the sons, until David came in.

"And the Lord *said, "This is the one; anoint him."*

So as David stood there among his brothers, Samuel took the flask of olive oil he had brought and anointed David with the oil. And the Spirit of the Lord *came powerfully upon David from that day on." (verses 16:12b-13)*

How many people right now are in a position or role because it was some person's idea or appointment (maybe even their own), and not God's? I've been in that situation myself! Interestingly however, God still worked with Saul in this position for a season, but as soon as Saul became willfully disobedient, the season was over.

I also think it's interesting to note that God values what's in our hearts. God looked into David's heart and saw courage, leadership and a love for the Lord. Each of these things helped make him a great king. What virtues are in your heart that will help you in your calling?

Next, you'll need to - ***Gain the confidence, skill and mindset to live it.***

Did you know that it's not the most naturally gifted or talented people who succeed in life? No, it's those who are disciplined and determined to develop and share their gifts with excellence, and believe they can. *A person could be brilliantly gifted, yet leave their destiny on the table because of idleness, poor self-image or simply remaining oblivious to their calling.*

> A person could be brilliantly gifted, yet leave their destiny on the table because of idleness, poor self-image or simply remaining oblivious to their calling.

I want you to gain confidence. I want you to gain skill. I want you to have the right mindset. I want to see you live God's calling for you. Let's break this down for a moment. I propose that these three areas are like a three-legged table; minus any one of these things, it will not stay standing.

1. **Confidence** – Not that you have to be fully confident in yourself, but it's very important to be assured that you are called and that God is with you. Also, part of it is being willing to do something that may scare you or be uncomfortable at first!

2. **Skill** – It's the art of being good, or proficient at what you do. Do what you do, well. Being skilled makes a big difference in whether or not you will be effective.

3. **Right Mindset** – You may have confidence that you have been called and have amazing skills, but **without a mindset or self-image that tells you that "you can," you won't.**

As people living in this fallen world, we have a lot of work to do in the area of mindset. Most of us have a fair amount of negative self-talk at work inside our minds, as well as limiting beliefs that keep us

> Without a mindset or self-image that tells you that "you can," you won't.

living small. For us to be able to launch out into our calling, renewing our minds daily is a necessity.

*"Do not conform to the pattern of this world, but **be transformed by the renewing of your mind**. Then you will be able to test and approve what God's will is—his good, pleasing and perfect will."* – Romans 12:2 (NIV)

In the Growth section of this book, we'll revisit this verse from Romans, and the entire topic of renewing our mindsets. You might be surprised at just how important this step really is to effectively step out and take your place.

Finally, the last lesson for us will be to: ***Allow the continuing, refining work of God to conform me into the image of Christ.***

In Romans 8, Paul writes that God has predestined us to conform to the image of His son. In other words, we are meant to become more and more like Jesus as we spiritually mature. As believers, we know this won't be complete until we reach Heaven at the end of our natural lives. We look to Jesus as our perfect example to aim for, even though we will not attain perfection here in our earthly bodies.

"I don't mean to say that I have already achieved these things or that I have already reached perfection. But I press on to possess that perfection for which Christ Jesus first possessed me. No, dear brothers and sisters, I have not achieved it, but I focus on this one thing: Forgetting the past and looking forward to what lies ahead" – Philippians 3:12-13 (NLT)

Just know this: God takes each of us on a path to get rid of our flesh (our human nature of selfishness and sin). God says that no flesh shall glory in His presence. He desires that we be led by His Spirit, rather than by our natural desires. This comes through a relationship with Him and obedience to His commands.

He must increase in our lives, attitudes, behavior, words, decisions, character, perspectives, etc., while our own flesh must decrease bit by bit. It's a progressive cleansing of our hearts and minds as we're washed in the water of the Word.

You know you have been sanctified, right? To be "sanctified" means being cleansed, made holy and set apart for God's purposes. Yep, that's you!

Summary

Beyond knowing our God-given gifts, comes the knowledge of God's overall calling for our life. Our gifts fit into our calling. We have a lot to learn about who we are, and here are lessons we need to learn:

1. Learn who I am in Christ
2. Know what my gifts are
3. See the calling God has for me
4. Gain the confidence, skill and mindset to live it
5. Allow the continuing, refining work of God to conform me into the image of Christ

These lessons are progressive, meaning each of these lessons builds upon the previous one(s).

Prayer: *Holy God, I thank You for your righteousness and holiness. You are amazing God, and I appreciate all that You do for me each day; even the things I don't even realize You are doing. You love me, even in my imperfection and shortcomings. You have been good to me. Teach me the way I need to go, and help me become more like You.*

Ask yourself:

- Is my confidence in me, or in God's power?
- What positions of leadership or responsibility do I occupy? Are they man-made appointments, or God-ordained?
- Are there promises from God to me that I do not currently experience?

Affirmations:

I know who I am – I am the Lord's!
My confidence is in the Lord and His plan for me.
Day by day, I learn to walk in the Spirit more and more.
I focus on what is ahead, because God has a good future planned for me.
I am sanctified – set apart for God's purposes.

Now it's time to learn more about your spiritual gifts. Are you ready?

6.

Spiritual Gifts – The Foundation
of Your Everyday Calling

Although this book is not meant to be a deep, comprehensive study of the spiritual gifts listed in the Bible, I want to take a moment to discuss and clarify them. The spiritual gifts that God has given you play a foundational role in His calling for you. They also play a very significant role in the church and world today.

You have spiritual gifts from God. They're an important part of your calling. These spiritual gifts enhance and work together with other natural gifts and abilities that God has given you. For example, here is a story from my friend, Jevon Bolden:

I have taken spiritual gifts tests on a few occasions and I have learned that I have the gifts of teaching, exhortation, wisdom, knowledge, and faith. What I was told I could do with these is teach Sunday school, encourage a friend who may be down, speak words of knowledge and wisdom to people during prayer and deliverance kinds of ministry, pray for someone to be healed because of my faith, etc.

Yes, I agree that is good and that is what I have done, but little did I know that my passion for literature, art, and music could also be enhanced through these same gifts. Because of that revelation, the glory of God is displayed in everything I do.

Now, I am a book editor and a worship leader and my gifts are displayed by me coaching and encouraging authors, developing plans and organizational structures for their abstract thoughts and ideas about how to reach people with their messages. I also mentor singers and musicians. I teach voice and how to worship. I mentor young adults (for some reason they are just attached to me).

Can you see how spiritual gifts collaborate with other gifts in life? This is an important correlation for each of us to make. In total, there are approximately twenty-eight (Bible scholars can't quite agree) unique spiritual gifts that are found in the Bible. To learn more about spiritual gifts, read 1 Corinthians 12, Ephesians 4 and Romans 12. I've included every gift that was mentioned during my research.

Here is a list and brief explanation of gifts discussed in the Bible:

Ministry Gifts (a.k.a. The 5 Fold Ministry):

- Apostle/Apostolic
- Prophet/Prophecy
- Evangelist/Evangelism
- Pastor/Pastoral
- Teacher/Teaching

You may have heard the term "the 5 fold ministry" before. It describes the five main positions of church leadership. They are specifically for use in, and for building up, the body of Christ.

Manifestation or "Charismatic" Gifts:

Spoken manifestations:
- Prophecy
- Speaking in tongues
- Interpretation of tongues

Action manifestations:
- Faith
- Healing
- Miracles

Revelation manifestations:
- Word of Wisdom
- Knowledge
- Discerning of Spirits

These are a category of gifts called "charismatic gifts." Spiritual gifts in this category are thought to be manifestations of the Holy Spirit at work through willing believers as needed, and when needed.

Serving Gifts:

- Administration
- Encouragement (speaking gift)

- Exhortation (speaking gift)
- Giving
- Helps/Serving
- Hospitality
- Intercession/Prayer
- Leadership
- Mercy/Compassion

Misc. Gifts:

- Craftsmanship
- Music
- Missionary (may be related to leadership/ministry gifts)
- Voluntary Poverty
- Voluntary Celibacy
- Interpretation of Dreams

These last two categories of gifts encompass many other important gifts found in various places in the Bible.

Spiritual Gift Personal Stories

For some of you reading this, it will be the first time you've ever heard the concept of spiritual gifts. This is very common! I have a friend named Derrick Miles who was a regular church attender for years, although didn't find out about His spiritual gifts until he was thirty-seven years old. Once he learned more about them, including his main gift, it literally changed his life. Here is what he has to say:

I must admit it...I fell for the corporate lie hook, line and sinker. As a young Christian, I was told that you go to college, obtain a good job, earn a good living and you will experience the finer things that life has to offer. Because of my inner drive, I took each one of those statement to the next level. I didn't get just one degree; I secured three. Not only did I earn a good living; my family was in the top 10% of wage earners in America. However, I didn't experience the finer things that life had to offer. My life was filled with insecurity, pride and borderline depression.

I noticed my heart beginning to change each time I took another corporate executive position to make more money. As the years went on, my desire to help others grow superseded my desire for year-end bonuses. Everything came to a climax when my father had a discussion with me about my work habits. He witnessed me getting up before the sun came up, driving 45-minutes into the city, working 10-12 hours, driving another 45-minutes home, eating dinner and falling asleep without spending any quality time with my family. His comment to me was, "Derrick, this life you living ain't worth a darn" (I'm being nice here). Normally, I would debate with my father, but this time I had no rebuttal. He was right! I thought, "There must be more to life than this."

Throughout my corporate career, I was always the most sought after mentor in the organization; not because I was the best leader, but because my gift of encouragement. Sharing my spiritual gift gave others the courage to pursue their own assignment, purpose and destiny. Honestly, I didn't know I had the spiritual gift of encouragement until a colleague told me that I had it. I had read Proverbs 18:16 many times (A man's gift will make room for him and bring him before great men), but no one ever taught me that I had a specific spiritual gift and how it would make room for me.

In May of 2009, God visited my bedroom and said, "It's time for you to speak for Me now." That comment overwhelmed me. For years I had practiced my communication skills, and had finally reached the point where I was receiving recognition for this skill set. But like Moses, my response was, "Are you sure you have the right guy? I'm about to become Chief Operating Officer of a hospital." His response was, "That won't happen. Will you accept the assignment?"

"Assignment" was a strong word choice to me. Because I had spent time reading the Parable of the Talents, I knew the outcome if I chose not to use what the Master had provided me. As a result, I responded in the affirmative. My next question to God was, "What do you want me to speak about?" He responded, "The gifts that I have put into my children because they do not know." It was finally coming all together for me! Someone told me about the gift I didn't know that I had, and so I was called to turn around and teach others about theirs.

After accepting the assignment, God has shown me the power of Proverbs 18:16. The power of your spiritual gifts reveal themselves when you know your specific gift and utilize it daily. I've traveled to countries and met world leaders I never thought would ever know my name.

My journey has brought me joy and fulfillment. Through study on this topic, God has led me to create a book series, CD series, radio program, blog and t-shirts to increase the awareness about the power of using spiritual gifts. My gift has definitely made room for me, and it's awesome having the opportunity to help others experience joy and fulfillment when they know and use their spiritual gifts daily.

Derrick has embraced his top spiritual gift so much, that he is now known as Derrick "The Encourager!" Once you start utilizing your gifts, not only will you perform better at work, in your community and at home, but you are so much closer to the ultimate assignment that God has put into your heart.

Another woman on a similar mission is radio show host and Christian life coach, Nicole Kirksey. Nicole says it's time for all of us to know our gifts and know our ministry. Of course, I agree! She works individually with people who want to know more about spiritual gifts and leadership. Here is her story:

When I was a new Christian, I read a book called <u>Know Your Ministry</u> by Bible teacher and pastor, Marilyn Hickey. The pocket-sized book explained the Romans 12 ministry gifts in detailed yet easy-to-digest bites. Marilyn paints clear word pictures of each of the gifts, and how these look when people are operating in them.

Reading that book sparked a God-given passion in me: to encourage and equip others for ministry and service. I named my business ministry Foundational Gifts, after the name that Marilyn gave for the Romans 12 gifts she described in her book.

Spiritual gifts are God-given, supernatural abilities—different from our talents, learned skills, and natural abilities. These spiritual gifts enable ordinary believers like you and me to be able to minister to other people in extraordinary ways. Using our gifts in the ways they were created and for the purposes they were designed helps to advance the causes of the Kingdom of God.

In order to be effective in serving and in advancing the Kingdom, we have to know what gifts God has given to us individually. Those gifts will help us determine how and where we can best serve in ministry.

As the word of God tells us to operate faithfully and boldly in our gifts (1 Peter 4: 10-11; 2 Timothy 1:6-7), the world would tell us that we should not. Why might we hold back from operating fully in our gifts, and stepping into God's call of ministry on our lives? Rejection, comparison and fear.

Sometimes, we reject the gifts that God has given us. We rate them as inconsequential in comparison to the gifts that other people have, and we may believe that they're not special, important, or good enough.

I myself have struggled greatly with confidence in one of my spiritual gifts, which is worship. I pray and I sing, and people are drawn into a more intimate encounter with God. It is a near-daily battle not to compare my vocal offerings to those of my powerhouse ministry partners, or the style of my prayers to those of faithful and experienced intercessors. For many years, I kept my singing and my praying to myself—out of fear that these would be rejected by others. Now, I realize that singing, praying, and worshiping in other ways are passions and empowerments that God has given me to help others, and I have a responsibility to do so. By faith, I believe that He is with me when I minister, and that my offering is acceptable to Him and to others.

It's so important that we know what our gifts are; what their definitions and uses are; and that get creative about ways that we can minister using our gifts. Ministry should be everywhere, not only in the church! Our communities, neighborhoods, schools, workplaces, business connections, and families should be experiencing the love of God through the use of our spiritual gifts on a daily basis.

Finding out which spiritual gifts you possess is an important part of your spiritual growth. It's also important information to have as you move forward in discovering how your gifts work together with your life as a whole.

Your church may have a spiritual gifts test available that you can take. Or, another option is to go online and take a spiritual gifts assessment. Actually, why not take a couple and compare the results. They're usually free! Please visit the Resources Section at the end of this book for links to recommended online assessments.

Special Note: When you take spiritual gifts assessments, answer the questions candidly. If you're anything like me, you may feel bad about how you answer some of the questions. Let me explain…

They will ask things like, "How concerned are you about the homeless population," "Do you desire to preach the gospel in remote locations" or "How often do you feel compelled to pray without ceasing?" Do not answer the assessment questions like you think they should be answered. "Well, I should care about this, so I will score myself highly in this area." If you do that, your results may not accurately reflect gifts you have, but qualities you wished you had. For correct results, simply answer them truthfully.

After you take them, print or write out the results for your top five spiritual gifts. You'll need this information for a practical exercise that is coming up in chapter 8.

Summary

Your spiritual gifts play a foundational role in the work God has for you. His overall calling for you involves the spiritual gifts He has chosen to give you. Each of His people has one or more spiritual gifts, to be used as the Holy Spirit directs.

There are approximately thirty spiritual gifts listed in the Bible, in several different types of categories. Visit Romans 12, Ephesians 4 and 1 Corinthians 12 to learn more about them.

God will use your spiritual gifts in collaboration with other aspects of who He has created you to be. An easy way to learn more about what spiritual gifts you have been given is to take a spiritual gifts test online or through your church. You can find out today what spiritual gifts you have!

Prayer: *Lord God, Your love and mercy endures forever! I see that You have made everything for Your glory, and I praise You for the remarkable gifts You have bestowed upon me. Help me use these gifts in a way that brings glory to You. Thank You for using me in my imperfection.*

Ask yourself:

- What are my top five spiritual gifts?
- Do I use my spiritual gifts on a daily basis? In what way?
- Is there anything else I would like to investigate further about spiritual gifts?

Affirmations:

God's Spirit is working within me and through me.
God's love and power thrives inside me, and I allow it to flow out to others.
My spiritual gifts are with me all the time, not just at church.

7.
Calling Components™

In each of our lives, there are a lot of things working together to serve God's purposes. I call them our Calling Components™. Think about it: Do you think it's a coincidence that you have this unique set of elements existing inside you?

1. Spiritual Gifts
2. Personality
3. Interests
4. Passions
5. Natural Abilities/Talents
6. Dreams
7. Past Experiences
8. Positioning

This concept may be new to you. It was to me when God revealed it to me. You may have never thought about all of these aspects of who you are as playing a part in God's calling for your life. Yes! It's not only about what your spiritual or natural gifts are, but also how, in what way, where, why you express them, and to whom you express them to.

On our Calling Components™ list, spiritual gifts have already been covered in the previous chapter. Next, I'd like to individually discuss each of the other components as well.

Personality

Personality – a common word, but what does it mean, exactly? Your personality is a compilation of the characteristics unique to you, such as your;

- temperament,
- communication style,
- traits,
- individuality,

- mannerisms,
- disposition,
- natural tendencies,
- attitudes,
- responses and reactions,
- sense of humor (or lack of),
- outlook (optimistic/pessimistic),
- level of expressiveness,
- likes and dislikes,
- adaptability or flexibility to different environments, etc.

In part, our personality is the sense, or impression, that others get about us as we interact with them and our environment. In addition to what others observe on the surface, I believe our personality lives inside our mind and thought processes as well. We have an outlook on life that exists inside our minds, that eventually works its way out, shaping what people observe about us.

Personality is the most commonly discussed aspect of who we are, yet one of the most difficult to define. During my research, I have found dozens of personality tests and types, which attempt to categorize people. Although personality tests are fun, interesting and sometimes enlightening, don't allow them to define who you are, or put you in a box. I do recommend taking personality tests during your journey to investigate yourself, but take them with a grain of salt! Simply collect data and contemplate it, without letting it label you.

Ask yourself:

- What type of personality do I have, or what are my biggest characteristics?
- How is God able to use my personality for His purposes?
- Does my personality style allow me to interact well with others around me?

Examples of Personality Traits:

Outgoing, inhibited, shy, boisterous, logical, creative, emotional, easy going, friendly, loyal, sly, controlling, passive, leader, uplifting, flexible, ambitious, judgmental, analytical, bold, calculating, daring, cheerful, diplomatic, introvert, extrovert, gentle, courageous, humorous, deep, proud, etc.

Interests

Think about this: *God cares about everything.* He's interested in helping people with every good cause, all mission fields, skill to be learned, every injustice and problem that people face, etc.

> God cares about everything.

For example, God deeply cares about homeless families, ministering to those in jail, health care in Africa, justice, clean oceans, diversity, etc. He is even concerned about things like early childhood development, the healing of bodies, good financial planning, music, ways in which technology can help society, and nutrition. God literally cares about everything of value!

However, I only have a handful of things I deeply care about and am interested in. Some interests that I have make sense; I can trace their origins back to an event or experience in my life. Other things I'm interested in are just there without explanation, other than God must have placed them within me Himself.

You are much the same. There are things in your life that you deeply care about and are interested in; Topics which you are passionate about and that capture your attention. There are many other topics and issues that do not.

Why is this? If we are God's people, shouldn't we care about everything too? In theory that would be nice, but in reality, no. Our hearts and minds are not set up with the capacity to be passionately interested in everything.

God gives each of us special interests, concerns and passions so that we can be used as His hands and feet in those specific areas. He deposits various interests into each of us to make sure all of His interests in the world today are covered.

Imagine God holding an enormous vat of feathers in Heaven; each feather represents a cause, topic, care, or passion of His. He pours out the vat, and a small number of feathers fall to each person on the planet. Some of His interests have fallen to you.

There is one potential sticking point with this category – fruitless recreation or time-wasters. If possible, stay away from thinking your interests are things like "watching TV," "video games" or "checkers." Unless you're going to become a board game pro or TV star, these types of activities (if they consume much of your spare time) will not help you get any closer to your purpose. In fact, they work against your destiny.

If you find that you don't have any answers except fruitless entertainment activities (time-wasters, unproductive, mind-numbing, empty activities), that should serve as a red flag for you. Also, there are unhealthy or immoral "interests" that are not of God. You are what you eat. Your mind is chewing on some kind of "food" too, whether it is healthful or junk.

Ask yourself:

- What am I interested in, specifically?
- What do I care about?
- How do I spend my time, and what topics you I feel driven to learn more about?

Examples of Interests:

Babies learning to communicate
Alternative energy sources
Dog or cat nutrition
News and current issues
Creating beautiful indoor environments
Plants and gardening
Hair care and styling
Deafness
Working with horses
Singing
Dancing
Victims of sexual abuse
Fitness or weight loss
Making videos
Business marketing
Marriage communication skills
Honoring veterans
Writing praise songs
Storytelling
Dairy farming

Fishing
Cooking
Creating websites
Advocating for school children and education
Foster parenting
Bible prophecy
Chiropractic therapy
Law enforcement
Technology solutions
Basketball or sports training
Positive self-esteem of teenagers
Organic farming
Removing litter from local streams
Weddings
Woodworking or crafting
Capturing history through photography
Clothing or jewelry
Real estate investing

It's fairly easy to determine your interests. Some may be simply a hobby or pastime for you. Others are passions for you. The passions you have are no accident or coincidence.

Passions

Your passions go beyond the level of having an interest in a field, topic or subject. Sometimes, you lose sleep over them. Passions are like interests on steroids!

Special note: One worldly definition of the word passion relates to sexual desire, which is in no way applicable to this discussion. Passions in your life that are from God, come from a pure-hearted place. "For the grace of God has appeared that offers salvation to all people. It teaches us to say "No" to ungodliness and worldly passions, and to live self-controlled, upright and godly lives in this present age" (Titus 2:11-12 - NIV). Worldly, sinful passions enslave us, rather than setting us free into God's calling for us.

The main separator between an interest and a passion is that emotions are attached to your passions. Passions are deep things you're driven and motivated by. When you're passionate about doing something, you're compelled to continue doing it because you love it.

For instance, if you have a time period where you're unable to work on a project that you're passionate about, you might feel "dry" inside. In order to truly be you and express your uniqueness, you must honor your passions. You'll continue to do these things because you love to, and if you were unable to for some reason, something would be missing.

Can you see the importance of this component? Passions motivate you. You feel driven by them. They are the deep desires of your heart that help you express your core essence.

Personally, I feel very passionate about others stepping out into their God-given callings, about creativity, about using sign language during worship, and about collaboration within the community of Christian business owners. What do you feel passionate about?

Krista Dunk

Ask yourself:

- What activities or topic(s) am I devoted to?
- What never feels like work when I spend time on it?
- What drives, or motivates me?

Examples of Passions:

Worship, counseling, parenting, supporting a cause, intercessory prayer, planning ministry events, helping others succeed, spiritual and personal growth, creating with your hands, preaching the gospel, feeding others, foster care, alternative medical solutions, environmental work, etc.

Natural Abilities (a.k.a. Talents or Gifts)

While God was knitting you together in your mother's womb, He knew you. Part of God's knitting you together process included building certain natural abilities, or talents, into you. These abilities are things you're naturally good at, and you probably always have been. These things come easily to you.

Many times, talents and natural abilities are referred to as a person's gifts. It makes sense, since like spiritual gifts, they're abilities that God specifically gave you, and which you are responsible for. You are a steward of your gifts. I imagine God places these abilities within us and then says, "Take good care of these gifts, develop them, cherish them, and be ready to use them as I instruct."

"Each of you should use whatever gift you have received to serve others, as faithful stewards of God's grace in its various forms." – 1 Peter 4:10 (NIV)

You can certainly develop your in-born talents further, creating expertise and advanced skill. There are many references in the Bible about how valuable "the work of skilled hands" is to God. Later in this book, there is a section specifically about developing your special abilities, or gifts.

"Tell all the skilled workers to whom I have given wisdom in such matters that they are to…" – Exodus 28:3a (NIV)

"Do you see someone skilled in their work? They will serve before kings; they will not serve before officials of low rank." – Proverbs 22:29 (NIV)

54

Part of determining what your natural abilities are is figuring out where your creativity lies. You might be thinking "I'm not one of those creative-type people," since most of the time being creative refers to people with artistic, musical or theatrical talent. However, that's not the case. You, too, are a creative person. Yes, really! Each of us has creative power in some area, or in several areas.

Maybe you don't have musical talents or artistic ability, but to you, brainstorming business ideas and solutions might be a snap. My husband has a huge amount of creativity in the area of technical solutions and ideas. Somehow, all that makes sense to his brain! I have a friend who can look at a piece of bare land and know exactly how it should be landscaped, and what it will look like 10 years later. Another friend can write a customized poem for a special occasion, and bring its reader to tears. Teacher Irene, my children's preschool teacher, can capture the enthralled attention of 12 preschoolers simultaneously with her storytelling ability. A CPA friend of mine has some of the most creative ideas about financial investing that I've ever heard.

It's funny, but often you have natural talents that slip under your own radar. It surprises you when other people take note of these things, because you've just assumed it's no big deal. Everyone can do that, right? Nope!

Ask Yourself:

- What abilities do I have that are easy for me, but not necessarily easy for others?
- What have people told me I'm good at?
- In what area(s) am I creative?

Examples of Natural Abilities/Talents:

Singing, written communication, mechanically inclined, drawing, connect well with kids, horticulture, working with animals, building things, comedy, theatrical, problem solving, organization, an eye for detail, sports, storytelling, decorating, easily learning multiple languages, etc.

Dreams

I liken this Calling Component™ to a visionary who has a picture of a better future. We all recognize this visionary's dream:

"I have a dream, that one day on the red hills of Georgia, the sons of former slaves and the sons of former slave owners will be able to sit down together at the table of brotherhood." – Dr. Martin Luther King Jr.

Inside each of us, there is the hope of better things to come, a shift or awareness that needs to happen or a truth that must be told. In Dr. King's case, he had a dream for our country, for unity of all diverse people, for renewed mindsets, and for society as a whole. This dream aligned with God's will. The dreams inside our hearts that are from God will always align with His will.

Investigating the dreams you have for your own life is another facet of your dreams category work.

Maybe it is related to the legacy you want to leave.
Maybe it's related to a personal accomplishment.
Maybe it's a goal your family has.
Maybe it's a dream related to one of your passions.
Maybe it's a dream to see a certain group of people's lives improved in some way.

Whatever it is, the life dreams you have are important. They say something about what you value.

Do you have dreams? If not, I bet you did once. *Dreams are tied to hope.* You may need to seek God and ask Him to unearth dreams that have become buried or have faded. Also, you may have old dreams that are appropriate to let go of because God has placed new ones on your heart.

> Dreams are tied to hope.

Ask yourself:

- If I were to declare, "I have a dream…" what would my dream be for the world around me?
- What life goals do I have for myself?
- Do I have dreams that have gone dormant?

Examples of Dreams:

Becoming an elected official, seeing addicts stop abusing drugs, ridding the world of child abuse, coach a winning sports team, leading thousands of people to Christ through speaking, writing a book, teaching children to express themselves through theatre, building up marriages, getting a degree, etc.

Past Experiences

As you can imagine, past experiences in your life play a role in who you are today. To some degree, significant events from your past (positive or negative) have impacted who you are now. It's very possible that some of the passions you have now stem from a past experience.

Past experiences that we will talk more about include:

- Significant, negative experiences in your past
- Significant, positive experiences in your past
- Past work experience and skills you have attained

I don't want to assume things about your past, but I know that many people have had some seriously negative experiences in their lifetimes. Maybe you have too. It reminds me of Joseph's experience of betrayal, hardship and God's favor.

> *"Then Joseph said to his brothers, "Come close to me." When they had done so, he said, "I am your brother Joseph, the one you sold into Egypt! And now, do not be distressed and do not be angry with yourselves for selling me here, because it was to save lives that God sent me ahead of you." –* Genesis 45:4-5 (NIV)

What Joseph's brothers meant for evil, God used for good. God can use your past pain for your future good and also to give others hope. *God can and will use everything for His glory; everything that you allow Him to heal.* He loves for His people to share their stories of faith, going from struggle to victory. Once we've come out victorious on the other side, we speak with authority because we've lived it. This helps others know what's possible for their lives too.

> God can and will use everything for His glory; everything that you allow Him to heal.

Also, as we see with Joseph, past experiences can actually move us in the right direction - towards our calling. I have a friend who was fired from a mediocre job, and was devastated. Another employee

57

didn't like her and made complaints, which got her fired. She was upset and confused, until two weeks later when a fabulous opportunity came along. If she hadn't been fired, she wouldn't have looked for or received this great, new blessing. Yes, it seemed bad at first, but it was a true blessing in disguise.

In the same way, if Potiphar's wife hadn't falsely accused Joseph of mistreatment and not had him sent to jail, he wouldn't have had the opportunity to interpret Pharaoh's dream and become a high-ranking official in Egypt.

The biblical story of Ruth is another good example. Ruth's husband died and left her with nothing. Being destitute and alone, she clung to her mother-in-law, Naomi's side. Her whole world was turned upside-down, but through a series of God-lead events, Ruth re-married and ended up being in the bloodline of Jesus. Talk about an exciting calling!

Even as God's people, we can experience serious hardship. Thankfully, God's plan always prevails if we trust and remain faithful to Him. Your calling may have something to do with a past negative experience that God has seen you through.

Past positive experiences can be meaningful to your calling too.

My brother-in-law, Aaron, is adopted. For him, he counts that as a positive experience in his life. Because of this, there is a special place in his heart for adoption in general. Since this is something he cares deeply about, he serves as a board member for a non-profit adoption agency.

In the Bible, both the apostle Paul and Esther had positive, meaningful experiences that linked to their God-given callings. Paul had a miraculous revelation from the Lord on the road to Damascus. The vision and message from the Lord instantly changed him. From that moment on, Paul became one of the most effective ministers of the Gospel this planet has ever seen.

Esther was a young woman chosen to live in luxury, as one of King Xerxes' wives. She eventually disrupted a plot to destroy the Jews in her kingdom. Additionally, near the end of the book of Esther, it says that new Jewish customs were established to be observed for generations to come because of this victory.

Some of my own past positive experiences include dreams and messages from God. They have impacted me in powerful ways, and have been related to His calling for me. Pay close attention to anything God shows or speaks to you.

In a lesser way, this component category could also include past skills learned, previous employment or career work. Through jobs you've had and vocational skills you've learned thus far in life, you bring that know-how with you. This know-how might be something useful to God.

Looking back on my work experiences, I can see how every job I've had built on the one before, and prepared me for the next position. As one skill set was learned, it expanded my capacity and provided a foundation for the next level.

I want to leave you with this thought for this Calling Component™: Through significant life experiences, God gives us a message to impart to others. If we pay attention to how God is using us to impact others, I believe each of us has a life message we're meant to share.

Ask yourself:

- What significant, past experiences have I had in my life? How did they change me?
- Do I have a message or wisdom for others because of something I've experienced in life?
- Do I have any passions that stem from a past experience?

Examples of Past Experiences:

A significant accomplishment, having suffered abuse, a tragedy or loss, miraculous healing, a circumstance you've overcome, addiction, adoption, a revelation or vision from God, divorce, starting a business, mission trip, mastering a skill, wartime military service, etc.

Positioning

This component is called positioning, and I believe it's often overlooked. Positioning has to do with the placement of our physical selves, today. It includes things like, where you live, the family you were born in to (or raised in), your neighborhood, the church congregation you belong to, where you work, what industry you're in, people you're in relationship with (friends, spouse, kids, network, etc.), which generation you belong to, etc.

Where you're positioned in life is something to take note of. God may have you in those places as a part of your calling. Looking at Esther's life again, she's a great example of how God used experiences and events to position her in the palace. When a great crisis came against the Jewish people in their kingdom, her uncle, Mordecai, had this to say to her:

> *"For if you remain silent at this time, relief and deliverance for the Jews will arise from another place, but you and your father's family will perish. And who knows but that you have come to royal position for such a time as this?"* – Esther 4:14 (NIV)

As we see in the book of Esther, God strategically positions people to do His work and further His purposes in situations and in people's lives. Like Esther, *God has people that you are assigned to influence.*

> God has people that you are assigned to influence.

Several phrases strike me about the scripture in Esther chapter 4. One is, "…if you remain silent… relief and deliverance…will arise from another place," and the other is, "…for a time such as this."

As we've already talked about, in Esther chapter 4, the story unfolds of an evil plot that's coming against God's people. It's interesting that Mordecai says that even if Esther remains silent now, that God's purposes will eventually prevail no matter what, although she and her own family will perish.

There's an important lesson here for each of us. It tells me that we play a very important role where we are positioned, and in the lives of those whom God has assigned for us to influence. God's purposes will be fulfilled, no matter what, but without our obedience in the here and now, someone (maybe even ourselves) suffers.

God strategically positioned Esther with influence in the palace…for a time such as that. As His hands and feet, we're also strategically positioned in our families, neighborhoods, work places, churches, social circles, cities, etc. All around us, there are others who are waiting for relief or for the Lord to deliver them in some way.

Lastly, the phrase "royal position" also catches my eye. Although you and I may not wear physical crowns, we have royal positions; positions where we've been given authority by the King of Kings.

Have you ever wondered why *you* are here, alive in this generation, right now, in your particular career, industry or workplace, in your neighborhood, in your specific family, and in your particular city? Esther had a call related to her specific time, location, relationships, and heritage. I believe each of us do as well.

I met a man from Pakistan who leads a Bible-based ministry. As you may know, Pakistan is a Muslim country. God has strategically placed Evangelist Qaiser Ijaz there, for this time, with a message of His love and salvation through Jesus. Here is what Qaiser has to say about his work there:

Passion of Christ Ministries Pakistan concentrates on children, widows, poor, etc., and has the vision to proclaim the Word of God among them. If you want to see the miracle, then be the miracle.

Pray and ask God to show you what all of these special placements in your life mean, and how they fit His purposes. I really do believe He's placed people in our lives that we're meant to positively influence (help, teach, support, pray for, care for, rebuke, inspire, lead, share with, advocate for, speak the truth to, etc.) in some way.

Ask yourself:

- Who am I in relationship with, and why? Could God have positioned me with them for a reason?
- What workplace, career or industry am I in? Why am I there?
- How have I been strategically placed, or positioned, by God?

Examples of Positioning:

Your geographical location (city/community you live in), family of origin, ethnicity, the people you're in relationship with, workplace, church body, neighborhood you live in, your generation, your leadership roles, etc.

Calling Component™ Combinations

Now that we've covered and defined each Calling Component™, let's take a look at a couple hypothetical people with different component combinations.

Heather

Spiritual gifts - teaching, helps/serving, administration
Personality - shy, generous, expressive
Interests - cooking, writing, outdoors
Passions - the humane treatment of animals, education, imparting a love for all life
Natural abilities - art, painting, organizational skills, inspiring others
Dreams - to open a wildlife refuge/shelter, to write a book, wants to visit Australia
Past experiences - loss of a child, won 4-H competitions as a youth, inherited land, had a profound dream from the Lord three years ago about children and animals
Positioning - age fifty, board member of a non-profit organization, works for city government, attends church in a nearby rural area, belongs to an artist's group in her community, is of Hispanic heritage

Hypothetically, Heather's everyday calling might look something like this:

- Through programs, creative writing and/or art, teaching children about how to care for animals and other creatures.
- Working at a zoo, animal shelter or rescue facility where she is able to welcome and teach the public about animal care.
- Teaching the value of life through creating educational curriculum for schools, churches, etc.

Her life's message might be: *Sharing a love for, and teaching others to care for, all life.*

Douglas

Spiritual gifts - teaching, leadership, administration
Personality - bold, compassionate, optimistic
Interests - history, war strategy, studying leaders
Passions - working with teenagers, patriotism
Natural abilities - verbal communication, memorization, good with tools
Dreams - to participate in a Civil War re-enactment, to uncover or discover a war-time secret, speaking at the White House, for every youth to have confidence and opportunity in life

Past experiences - chosen as a camp counselor as a young adult, won an award as a speaker, past military service, father abandoned his family when Douglas was fourteen

Positioning - age thirty, lives in a big city, from a family with several generations of teachers and/or military servicemen, newlywed, in college, has a lot of active duty military friends

Possibilities for Douglas' everyday calling might include:

- Bringing his passion for teens and history together, as a high school history teacher.
- Consulting and speaking as a historical events expert.
- Serving as a youth group leader, who brings biblical battles to life.

His life's message might be: *Leading others successfully through life's battles,* or *showing the next generation how to live in service to God and country.*

Also, please visit chapter 20 where I discuss the outline of my calling.

Can you see how these two people, both with teaching and administrative spiritual gifts, can be so different? Do you see how each combination of characteristics adds up to create something quite unique? Do you see how God has purposely made us different, and uses this variety to serve His purposes on earth? There's a valuable richness found in diversity, which makes us so useful to God and to one another.

Take time to reflect, pray and meditate on this information. In the next chapter, we'll review the practical application information about how to seek God for His plan for your life.

Special Note: Now that we've examined all your Calling Components™ and strengths, I feel compelled to tell you this: Part of God's calling for your life may include areas where you feel weak or inadequately skilled. Don't be surprised if He has you share your gifts in a way that requires complete reliance on Him, and without Him it won't work out.

He loves that, because He gets the glory and your faith increases. For example, my calling involves public speaking. Truly, I *never* saw myself with that gift, and it still requires much dependence on God. At one point, He told me, "Your weakness is the strength. I show Myself strong."

Each time I speak, I cannot claim to have confidence in myself, only the confidence in knowing what God has called me to do. He spoke, I listened, I trusted, I got ready, and I stepped out.

Summary

As you can see, you are quite complex! There's a lot to you, and all of these pieces are working together for some kind of God-purpose. You know that you're one-of-a-kind, right? I bet that no one else has ever had, or ever will have, the exact same set of Calling Components™ as you do. You are a unique instrument!

Spiritual Gifts – Your God-given, spiritual gifts are a foundational piece of your overall calling and of the good work assigned to you. "There are different kinds of gifts, but the same Spirit distributes them" (1 Corinthians 12:4).

Personality – Personality is made up of your in-born temperament as well as traits you've developed while maturing. Your distinct personality plays a key role in how you interact with others around you. It also has an influence on how you express your gifts.

Interests – You have certain interests, hobbies and things you enjoy spending your time and effort on. God always has someone interested in, and paying attention to, the things He cares about.

Passions – They're the deep desires of your heart that help you express your core essence. Your passions have emotion attached to them, and you feel driven and motivated by them. Pay attention to the things you have zeal for! They may be related to your calling.

Natural Abilities – Natural abilities are otherwise known as talents or gifts. They're to be expressed and shared with others. You have certain things that you're naturally good at, and they come easy to you. This is not a coincidence! God made you with these gifts for a reason.

Dreams – Dreams could be life goals. Dreams could also be your version of what a perfect world would look like. For example, Dr. Martin Luther King Jr. had a dream.

Past Experiences – Whether positive or negative, your past experiences may be useful to God. Your story of overcoming, victory or lessons learned could be part of God's calling for you.

Positioning – God strategically positions people to do His work and to further His purposes in situations and in people's lives. Take note of the various ways you're positioned in life, right now, including where you live, your generation, your ethnic group, leadership roles, workplace, etc.

Take the time to meditate upon each of your components, and it will help you better understand your exceptional design.

Prayer: *Lord, You are so wise! I see that I am fearfully and wonderfully made by Your hands. I am Your design! Speak to my mind and thoughts and bring things to my remembrance. I want to understand my special design. May Your purposes prevail.*

Ask yourself:

- Are there any common themes that keep coming up as I examine my Calling Components™?
- Do I understand how the components blend together for God's purposes in my life?
- In what way(s) am I creative?

Affirmations:

Every piece of who I am is God's design.
I am a creative person.
I find passion and purpose in life by using my gifts.
I wisely spend my time on activities that bring me Godly wisdom and joy.

8.

Practical Discovery Strategies - The Outer Work

I would like to begin this chapter with a story from a friend, Marnie Swedberg. Marnie is a minister to women, an author, wife, business owner, and beautiful woman of God. She's someone that God uses in a powerful way to impact the lives of the people around her.

Since I was a young teen, I have been a mentor to women. At age fourteen, I helped with the four-year-old Children's Church group, but that was just the beginning. By my mid-twenties, I was hosting Bible studies for young girls in my home. Later I started the Amah-El Club for girls and also hosted a women's Bible study. I went on to serve as the president of our women's group at church for nearly twenty years.

But the concept of a mission or vision was foreign to me for much of that journey. It began to take shape one day in my early thirties when I was working in my kitchen. As I worked and talked with God, three phrases came into my thoughts: 1) encourage women, 2) provide them with practical help, and 3) turn their thoughts toward Jesus.

The thoughts would not go away, so finally I grabbed a 3x5 recipe card, wrote them down and taped the card to the inside of a cupboard door.

As the years went by, I would see that card from time to time, but it wasn't until I read Laurie Beth Jones' book, The Path, that I understood what God had given me that day.

My little 3x5 from God was my mission statement. My vision is to do everything God created me to do in and through His power for His glory. But my mission, the "how I go about it," is to encourage women, provide them with practical help and turn their thoughts toward Jesus.

The practical out-flowing is manifold in my life:

- *My restaurant provides nutritious foods for gals who are too busy to cook, while providing Christian music and kind staff to encourage her while she waits. In doing so, to turn her thoughts toward Jesus, if she so desires.*

– *My books, songs, blog, speaking engagements, radio talk show, social networking posts and websites are all geared to accomplish these goals.*

– *Our family-owned retail store, which provides the practical things women need in a location near them, is staffed by many Christians who love and pray for the customers as they shop. We play Christian music and offer a wide selection of Christian books in our bookstore (including a section just for women).*

– *When I speak and consult, God, prayer and an eternal focus permeate my motivation, words and actions.*

No matter what decision I have to make about how to use my time, or how to invest myself once a decision is made, all naturally flows through the filters of my vision and mission statements. They are more than words. I see them as the blueprint of how God created me.

Trying to live my life without taking into consideration the God who created me and His specific plans when He built me "to spec" would be an exercise in futility. Living life by His plan, according to His purposes and through His empowerment, is pure joy.

As you can see, Marnie has taken a journey with God. She knows her gifts, and has stepped out and has taken her God-ordained place. Now it's your turn.

Are you ready to dig into some practical gifts and calling discovery strategies? In the previous chapter, you just read all about your various Calling Components™, so now it's time for the concepts and information to become real, actionable plans for you to move forward with.

In my estimation, *two types of work are required for us during this process: Outer work and inner work.* When you grow, there's always an outer work and an inner work to do. Let me explain the difference.

<u>Outer Work:</u> Outer work encompasses everything we can do in the natural realm; natural, physical, practical actions. For example, the actions that you

> Two types of work are required for us during this process: Outer work and inner work.

take that back up your prayers, people you talk to, classes and training, volunteering and serving, etc.

Inner Work: Inner work is the spiritual growth part of it, such as seeking, character development, renewing your mind, drawing near to God, prayer, etc. These are examples of the necessary "inner work" in the spiritual realm.

If you pay close attention, the principle of inner and outer work, or spiritual and natural realm work, applies in all growth areas of life. The most effective people I know understand these two realms and the attention (and actions) they require. Not sure what I mean? Look at these examples:

Example 1: Job Hunting

- ✓ Outer work would include filling out applications, making calls, scouring job listings, talking with your network of friends and connections, taking classes to brush up on skills.
- ✓ Inner work would include prayer to ask God to place you in the position He wants you in, and perseverance and faith that He will provide this perfect job at exactly the right timing.

Example 2: Adopting a Child

- ✓ Outer work would include learning about rules, procedures and regulations, preparing your home for an additional family member, connecting with adoption agencies, deciding where to adopt from, filling out necessary paperwork.
- ✓ Inner work would include prayer and fasting to seek God's will, studying the Bible to learn more about the spirit of adoption, preparing your heart for a child, renewing your mind and trusting the Lord.

Example 3: Believing God for Financial Help

- ✓ Outer work would include diligent work, disciplined spending, sticking to a new family budget, learning money tips and strategies from a mentor or financial counselor, continuing to tithe.
- ✓ Inner work would include asking God for creative ideas for generating income, renewing your mind about how you view money and keep a positive expectation to see God's hand work, prayer for wisdom, provision and insight.

As you can see in the situations above, inner work without outer work or vice versa, may not get you the desired outcome. In my own life, when circumstances are stuck, or there is confusion, I ask, "Lord, have I missed something, either in the spiritual or the natural? Teach me what I need to know. Show me what I can do." Sometimes, I've done all I can, and there is nothing else I can do but simply pray, trust and wait.

The inner work is done through faith, and the outer work is action taken based on that faith.

During the gift and calling discovery journey, it's no different. Inner and outer works are two sides of the same coin – the coin of finding God's plan. You do your inner and outer work, and God does the rest.

Here are seven practical (outer work) ways for you to discover more about your gifts, and to pursue knowledge about your calling. You can take action on these ideas right away.

1. Take Assessments and Tests
2. Complete a ME CHART™
3. Seek Wise Counsel
4. Serve
5. Get Mentors
6. Keep a Calling Discovery Journal
7. Keep This Book Open

Each one of these practical strategies helps bring the pieces of your puzzle into view. Let's dive more in-depth into each of these now.

1. Take Assessments and Tests

If you enjoy taking surveys, you will love this discovery strategy. It's a fun way to do research about who you are. Some tests are scientific, while others are more "fluffy" and just for fun. As you take them, evaluate the questions they ask and try to determine what's being evaluated. For example, some tests will evaluate your interests, some your mindset, some your natural abilities, and others your values.

Here are a few types of assessments and tests you can take in your discovery process:

• Personality Tests
• Spiritual Gifts Assessments

- Strengths Assessments
- Career Surveys
- Temperament Assessments
- Behavioral Style Tests

Sometimes, certain classes or workshops that that you take will offer assessments.

Special Note: Although many online assessments and tests are free (which is great), don't be surprised if ads clutter the screen along with your test. Free surveys attract a lot of site visitors, so sites offer them free and then sell ads to companies to make money.

During this book project, I researched quite a few types of surveys, tests and assessments. Below are some thoughts on a few of the testing categories.

Spiritual Gifts Assessments:

- There are a lot of online and written spiritual gifts assessments available. Start at your church. Is there a test they already have to offer? If not, do a search online for "free spiritual gifts tests" and see what results pop up. In the Resources Section of the book, there are several websites listed for you to try out.

  I recommend taking three of them, as not all of them have the same exact gifts that they test for and give results on. Hopefully you'll notice the same gifts coming up repeatedly in your top gift results. As I mentioned before, it's so important to answer them with complete honesty so your results are correct.

Personality Tests:

- One of the most popular and well-known personality tests available is the Myers-Briggs Type Indicator®. According to their research, there are sixteen different personality types. I have taken this test myself and it was interesting to get the results. Not only did it discuss strengths, but it also touched on potentially negative angles of the personality types as well.

- The DiSC® Profile personality assessment is another very popular test. Often, organizations, churches and companies use the DiSC® test for their workers or members to evaluate their work preferences and tendencies based on their behavioral styles. It also helps people understand the working styles of other individuals better, which hopefully improves overall teamwork. There's a fee associated with this testing system and often larger organizations get their testing materials in bulk.

Career Surveys:

- I've taken several career surveys in my lifetime, including one in high school, in college and another one recently. Although not perfect, they will give you something to think about. They normally measure how interesting you find different career options. It's just one more tool for us in the data collection process for self-assessing who we are.

  My most recent career survey from LiveCareer.com (which was filled with ads, but well worth the effort to get through to the results) seemed to match me very well, showing writing, leadership, artistic and teaching as my top areas of interest. Yep!

Temperament Test:

- ARNO Profile System™ (A.P.S.) is an assessment test that has been used by pastors and Christian counselors since 2000 to determine a person's in-born temperament or tendencies. Since personality tests can be more variable, depending on a person's mood, learned behavior or social setting, this one has less variability in results. You could probably take it at age ten and at age sixty and get the same results.

  I appreciate the A.P.S. test because of the unique results perspective it offers, and especially because it's faith-based. This test must be administered by a certified Christian counselor and has a fee associated with it. *(See the Resources Section)*

Once you've taken all these assessments and tests, you may be wondering what to do with the results. I have all my assessment and test results saved into one document on my computer. I can refer to it at any time, all in one place. Maybe you'd prefer to print out your results and keep it in a file folder, or write it all down in a journal or notebook.

Use the test data you collect as interesting evidence about you. Much of it will reveal your tendencies, interests and values. Something you could ask yourself is, "Do my actions and current situation in life match up with the results data?"

2. Complete a ME CHART™

In the previous Calling Components™ chapter, we talked about eight important aspects of who God has created you to be. In a nutshell, a "ME CHART™" is a written graph where you record all of your personal inventory answers for each of the eight categories.

Spiritual Gifts:	Personality:	Interests:	Etc...

Part of my journey of discovery involved creating this concept of a ME CHART™, and completing one for myself. After I had contemplated, prayed about and brainstormed these different areas, I filled in my ME CHART™ sections with everything that surfaced. I thought about each section separately, one at a time. I came up with several things in each category. Some of my answers were appropriate in more than one category.

Once my own ME CHART™ was complete, I noticed trends. I had a couple things showing up in several categories. You'll probably notice trends on yours as well. Circle the things that come up several times. Take note of them, as they represent something meaningful in your life.

Remember my story about God speaking to me, saying, "build up the body?" About a year after God inspired me with this ME CHART™ concept and I had completed my own, my husband and I were asked to lead our church small group through a study on life purpose. When we got to the end of that study, several group members were very frustrated that they still didn't understand God's personal plans for them.

I brought out my chart as an example of what they could do to help that discovery process, and they were astonished. They were amazed that I had created something like this, but to me it seemed like no big deal. It was at that moment that I realized people need more help in this area, and that my call to build up the body may have something to do with this.

I encourage you to create a ME CHART™ of your own. It's really exciting because once your chart is complete, you have pieces to a puzzle about yourself right there in front of you. At least you'll be able to see your puzzle pieces visually now!

Note: In the *Step Out and Take Your Place Companion Workbook*, there is a full-sized ME CHART™ for you to use as you contemplate all your Calling Components™, including more instructions.

3. Seek Wise Counsel

Hopefully you have a trusted friend or family member (or several) who you can speak freely and openly with, and who tells you the truth in love. People close to you, who have your best interests in mind, make wonderful, wise counsel. They've observed you for a long time, and they may be able to offer clues about your gifts and calling. When seeking their counsel, your goal is to ask them, "What do you see in me? What do you think my gifts are?"

However, be selective about who you allow to speak into your life. If you establish someone as an authoritative figure in your life, you give them a certain amount of power. With power, comes influence. Some people may offer unsolicited advice or opinions, but it doesn't mean you need to accept it. If a person's advice, opinions or suggestions do not align with God's Word or His truth, reject it.

Every day you get unsolicited advice and images filling your mind from the media, movies, TV, magazines, etc., about who you should aim to be. Most of the time, this is unwise counsel! Do not allow any guidance into your mind and spirit that is not of God.

Examples of wise counselors might be pastors, coaches, trusted friends and family who want to see God's best for you.

4. Serve

Volunteer in a variety of roles at your local church and/or in other organizations. Some of us learn best by trying things. When you experiment with serving in different capacities, you'll learn a lot about yourself. After you complete your ME CHART™, you may see indicators about what volunteer roles and opportunities would be best for you to test out.

I highly recommend *not* using serving as the lone option for discovering your gifts and calling, however. Use it in combination with the other spiritual and natural ideas that are listed. Why, you ask? Although serving can jump you right into action (and some of us really love diving right into action), skipping the other seeking methods can stunt this whole process.

Potential places to serve and volunteer at include churches, online ministries, non-profit organizations, PTSA's, on community committees, city projects, clubs, hospitals, food banks, through apprentice programs, sports teams, etc.

5. Get Mentors

With mentors, your goal is to learn from their example and experience. In our charge to "get wisdom," mentors play a big role in being sources of wisdom for us. Of course, our greatest mentor is the Holy Spirit. He teaches us directly from God's heart.

> *"But the Counselor, the Holy Spirit, whom the Father will send in my name, will teach you all things and will remind you of everything I have said to you."* – John 14:26 (NIV)

Mentors can also include many kinds of people, such as authors, business people, pastors, parents, advisors, educators, coaches, Godly counselors, etc.

When searching for a good mentor to learn from, you should look for people who are operating in their giftings and calling well already. Find wise, trustworthy mentors who challenge you, dig up your potential, tell you the truth, and encourage you to grow. They may also make you feel uncomfortable at times, and hold you accountable when you'd rather be a slacker. Mentors will also be vitally important during your gift development and gift sharing phases.

Many people can teach, inspire and motivate you with their books, messages and knowledge from afar, and that is good. However, the type of mentoring that is the most effective during your seeking phase offers a back-and-forth, personal dialogue and a personal relationship. This will ensure accountability and the personal help you need.

One of my mentors in life is Pastor Ray Frederick. He has helped my husband and I in the areas of finances, business and marriage. One of his passions is mentoring others, and I wanted him to share some of his advice and experiences:

Do you realize that God has placed people in your life to shape you? The younger you are, the more people are around to shape you. The older you are, the more people God brings into your life for you to shape them. God is persistent. We may try to brush some people off or push them away, but God usually sends a new person with the same mission!

A funny thing happens at some point in our lives. We notice that less people are coming to shape us, and more people are coming to be shaped. You're either on one end of that deal or the other. Right now, there are not as many people coming to help shape my life anymore. When you are young, be open. God has sent a gift to you, a relationship, to help shape your life.

I remember as a young married man, I thought I knew it all. After I was married, I realized I didn't know anything! Be open to those people who God will send. They are a gift. Those of us who are a little more mature, start looking around for those for you to shape. Those who refuse to be shaped cannot shape other people.

> Those who refuse to be shaped cannot shape other people.

Mentors are people who shape our personality and help us develop our skills. Be assured that God will send you challenging relationships; some that may even put you through the wringer. In the mid-70's I realized God was calling me to a teaching ministry. God has a sense of humor, because I was deathly afraid of talking or speaking to people. Being in front of people was more than I thought I could handle.

In 1980, I got hired by a radical pastor who has been one of the greatest teachers I've ever met in my life, and one of the greatest shapers of my ministry. I had the privilege of sitting under his leadership and example. I am still who I am, but my destiny was shaped because of this relationship. God sends mentors to you that will help form and shape you in the way God wants. He's not looking for clones, not looking for you to copy somebody else, but to help develop who God made you to be.

He will send people into your life to help shape you, so that you can experience God's best.

6. Keep a Calling Discovery Journal

Keeping a journal of messages you receive from God during this process is priceless.

Do you know why Old Testament saints built altars to the Lord after something great happened? So they would remember. The piled up rock altars created a visual reminder that the Lord had visited them, had spoken and had provided for and met their need.

> *"Then come, let us go up to Bethel, where I will build an altar*
> *to God, who answered me in the day of my distress and who has*
> *been with me wherever I have gone." –* Genesis 35:3 (NIV)

Keeping a journal is very much like your way of building an altar to the Lord, keeping track of what you are learning from Him, His blessings and the words He speaks to your heart. Seriously, keeping a journal like this is precious!

I have a journal where I keep track of everything God speaks to me, as well as other things I am learning during my inner work. It's one of my most prized possessions. My friend, author Lois Williams, is so proficient at journaling, that she teaches workshops on how to keep different kinds of journals for things like vision discovery, devotional time, prayers, healing, and gratitude journals.

Journals are a great way to capture information about yourself, and information from God to you.

> *Visit www.StepOutandTakeYourPlace.com to order*
> *your Gifts & Calling Discovery Journal.*

7. Keep This Book Open
Most people read through the first few chapters of a book, never to pick it up again. That fact doesn't bother me much, unless what's in the book can change a life or potentially change thousands of lives.

Your calling is so important, to you, to God and to the lives that you will influence. However, it's not an "easy button" process. God enjoys this journey with you. He will walk with you and talk with you, lead you and transform you.

Only you can make the decision to keep going. Make the decision to keep this book open so that you can *Step Out and Take Your Place* – your God-ordained place!

Summary

Two types of work are required for us during this process: Outer work and inner work. The outer work describes practical actions we can take in the natural realm, and inner work is what we do in the spiritual realm.

Outer work includes:

1. Take assessments and tests
2. Complete a ME CHART™
3. Seek wise counsel
4. Serve
5. Get mentors
6. Keep a calling discovery journal
7. Keep this book open

During the gift and calling discovery journey, inner and outer works are two sides of the same coin – the coin of finding God's plan. You do your inner and outer work, and God does the rest.

Prayer: *Living Water, Your grace is sufficient for me. I will enter Your courts with thanksgiving and give You praise! Give me the perseverance and desire to stay close to You. Holy Spirit, keep me connected to wisdom and truth. I love Your truth and wisdom Lord. Bless me with Your presence.*

Ask yourself:

- Am I willing to do these outer work steps?
- Who can mentor me in the direction God wants me to go?
- How will I keep track of all the information I receive?

Affirmations:

I am proactive about, and dedicated to, discovering what God has for me.
Today, I choose to move forward in my journey with God.
Every day I am learning new truths about myself.
God has sanctified me, and has set me apart for His purposes.

9.

Spiritual Discovery Strategies – The Inner Work

Now it's time to take a look at the second side of the seeking coin – The inner work. *Without doing the inner work, I can confidently say that you will not discover the fullness of God's calling for your life.*

As with the seven outer work strategies discussed in the previous chapter, there are also seven, inner work ways for you seek God. Just like with the natural seeking activities, you can also get started with these spiritual realm seeking activities right away:

> Without doing the inner work, I can confidently say that you will not discover the fullness of God's calling for your life.

1. Prayer and Meditation
2. Study the Bible
3. Worship and Praise
4. Find Biblically-Based Purpose, Vision and Calling Teaching
5. Fasting
6. Capture Rhema Words and Visions
7. Renew Your Mindset

1. Prayer and Mediation
Take the time to talk to God. God has the information you seek. He is your source. Strive to understand His heart for the people around you, your relationships, for your uniqueness, and for His purposes in the world.

Set a daily prayer schedule for yourself, and stick to that schedule. Seek Him in prayer and you will find Him. Build a relationship with the Father and He will teach you what you need to know through the Holy Spirit.

- Pray while you drive
- Pray while in the bathroom
- Start your day with prayer as you wake up
- End your day with prayer before you go to bed
- Use your lunch break to pray
- Write yourself prayer notes

- Pray as you read your Bible and pray God's promises out loud for yourself
- Pray right now!

"My sheep hear my voice, and I know them, and they follow me: And I give unto them eternal life; and they shall never perish, neither shall any man pluck them out of my hand." – John 10:27-28 (KJV)

My friend, pastor's wife Gail Dudley, has the spiritual gift of prayer intercession. She is so passionate about the topic, that she's written a book and conducts workshops to help people understand how to pray effectively. She has this quick advice and information to offer you, right now:

What is prayer? Prayer is having a conversation with God. It's talking to Him. It's sharing everything about you with Him. It's crying. It's laughing. It's going to God with your entire heart and talking and talking and talking. It's about coming away with His heart and trusting all He shared with you. It may be a word. It may be peace in your spirit. It may be a still small voice. It may be a scripture you have read. It may be silence. It's the time you and God share together, and then to sit still and bask in His presence.

Here's an example of prayer as you seek God's plans for your life. Often times we think we have to use long words and be extra deep - Not the case. Take a look at Jeremiah 29:11. It says, "For I know the plans I have for you," declares the LORD, "plans to prosper you and not to harm you, plans to give you hope and a future." We can take that scripture and pray it over ourselves like this: "God, you say in your Word that you know the plans you have for me; thank you, God for orchestrating my path, and for giving me a hope and a future. I trust you and I give my life to you, Lord. In Jesus' name, amen."

When we pray something that God agrees with or desires to see happen, these are powerful prayers. I image that God has plans He wants to implement, and is just waiting for someone to pray for His hand to move in that area. Right now, what could God be waiting for you to pray for?

2. Study the Bible

"As you study the scriptures, realize that God does not want to write to you; He wants to speak to you." – Pastor Dave Minton

Just like with prayer, set a daily time to read the Bible, and stick to that schedule every day. Your dedication to this shows God that you are serious, and He will bless that effort. He will teach you.

In fact, I believe that studying the Bible is one of the most important activities in this process. Want to have a good life? Want to understand all that God has for you? Go to the Bible.

Read – Study – Meditate – Practice

> *"Your word is a lamp to guide my feet and a light
> for my path."* – Psalm 119:105 (NLT)

That scripture is saying that God's Word illuminates and guides us on the right path. That's exactly what we need!

3. Worship and Praise

Worship is generally thought of as the singing portion of a church service, but it actually encompasses much more than that. For this inner work strategy however, I *am* speaking specifically about praising and worshipping God with music.

Music is a powerful tool that almost instantly affects a person's heart, thoughts, spirit, and mood. Some of the greatest revelations I've had spiritually, have been during times of worship (or right after). My step-dad likes to say, *"Worship is the breeding ground for the miraculous."*

> "Worship is the breeding ground for the miraculous."

Worshipping with music, instruments, singing and/or dance opens your heart and helps you express your heart openly, to have a mind freed from worry and to receive information from God all at the same time. Worshipping with music, song and dance also invites God's presence to draw near to you.

- Worship is a vehicle that allows you to enter God's presence
- Worship is refreshing
- Worship is intimate
- Worship renews your spirit

My sister, worship pastor Trisha Ferguson, is used powerfully by God to help others enter into God's presence through praise and worship music.

She has this to say about the power of worship, and how it can open you up to hear from God:

Praise and worship give us the unique opportunity to communicate our heart's passions to God. It is in those moments of true intimate worship and authoritative praise that God not only changes the natural, but creates the supernatural changes. The restorative power, the healing power, the wisdom and the rejuvenation that happens in those moments are exactly what God is gracing us with to move forward in His call on our lives. To truly find God, you have to release yourself in worship and you have to know the powerful effect of praising your Heavenly Father has.

There is tangible power in your expressive praise and worship time. Do you take advantage of that?

I don't know about you, but I used to be *very* inhibited during worship. I noticed other people who could truly express their hearts to God, and felt moved by the words they were singing. I didn't know what it meant or felt like to have freedom of expression in that way. I just stood, clapped and sang, unfortunately fitting in with the majority of the crowd. This was me:

"The Lord says: 'These people come near to me with their mouth and honor me with their lips, but their hearts are far from me. Their worship of me is based on merely human rules they have been taught.'" – Isaiah 29:13 (NIV)

This was an entire journey in itself for me, although I now know the journey and new freedom of expression has to do with God's specific calling for my life. Although it took many years to break out of my "worship shell," the difference is like night and day. I pray you, too, will find the place of freedom in worship to express your heart to the Lord.

One last thought about worship. In Deuteronomy 16, there is a verse that says, *"No one should appear before the LORD empty-handed."* What will you bring to Him in worship? Thanksgiving, praise, honor, a contrite heart, an offering?

4. Find Biblically-based purpose, vision and calling teaching
God tells us to get wisdom! If you read Proverbs chapters 4, 16, 17, 19, 21, and 23, they all have verses that implore us to get wisdom above all else. Like the workshop opportunities I offer, there are many wonderful

resources, teachings, sermons, and books available to help us understand how to discover our God-given gifts.

The information and lessons learned from pastors, teachers and business leaders will inspire and educate you. The wisdom from others that benefits you the most ultimately comes from God, through the Holy Spirit. Search for the Godly wisdom that others possess.

Note: Be sure that what you are feeding on is biblically-based. A lot of resources out there will have a sense of spirituality, but offer the wrong message. "It's all within you," is a message that infers that you are self-sufficient. We have a Designer. Trying to find our purpose and gifts apart from God your Designer will be another source of frustration and dissatisfaction.

"If any of you lacks wisdom, he should ask God, who gives generously to all without finding fault, and it will be given to him." – James 1:5 (NIV)

5. Fasting

Fasting takes prayer and Bible studying to the next level. At its most basic level, fasting is withholding something from yourself, usually some type of foods, food altogether or a habit or usual activity. Fasting is an extensive topic that I won't fully get in to here, but here are a few thoughts about doing it successfully:

1. Pre-set a few things in your mind, such as length of fast, what you will be fasting from and what the purpose is of your fast.
2. Deliberately fast from something that is tempting to you. If you despise all vegetables, and you decide to fast from vegetables... That is not a good plan!
3. Fast when you have an important upcoming decision to make, or are seeking answers for yourself or for a loved one.
4. Commit to it, even though your flesh will fight against it. That is the point exactly - to overcome your flesh and show God you are serious about seeking Him.
5. When temptation hits, pray right then about why you are fasting.
6. Be in positive expectation that you *will* hear from the Lord during the fast.

As an example, Esther fasted, and asked others to fast and pray before she went before the king. I am not a fasting expert, and don't claim to know how it all works in the spiritual realm. But I do know God sees and cares about the way we fast. This very interesting section of the Bible shows God's heart on this topic:

"Shout it aloud, do not hold back. Raise your voice like a trumpet. Declare to my people their rebellion and to the descendants of Jacob their sins. For day after day they seek me out; they seem eager to know my ways, as if they were a nation that does what is right and has not forsaken the commands of its God.

They ask me for just decisions and seem eager for God to come near them. 'Why have we fasted,' they say, 'and you have not seen it? Why have we humbled ourselves, and you have not noticed?'

"Yet on the day of your fasting, you do as you please and exploit all your workers. Your fasting ends in quarreling and strife, and in striking each other with wicked fists. You cannot fast as you do today and expect your voice to be heard on high.

Is this the kind of fast I have chosen, only a day for people to humble themselves? Is it only for bowing one's head like a reed and for lying in sackcloth and ashes? Is that what you call a fast, a day acceptable to the LORD?

> **You cannot fast as you do today and expect your voice to be heard on high.**

Is not this the kind of fasting I have chosen: to loose the chains of injustice and untie the cords of the yoke, to set the oppressed free and break every yoke? Is it not to share your food with the hungry and to provide the poor wanderer with shelter— when you see the naked, to clothe them, and not to turn away from your own flesh and blood?

Then your light will break forth like the dawn, and your healing will quickly appear; then your righteousness will go before you, and the glory of the LORD will be your rear guard. Then you will call, and the LORD will answer; you will cry for help, and he will say: Here am I.

"If you do away with the yoke of oppression, with the pointing finger and malicious talk, and if you spend yourselves in behalf of the hungry and satisfy the needs of the oppressed, then your light will rise in the darkness, and your night will become like the noonday.

The LORD will guide you always; he will satisfy your needs in a sun-scorched land and will strengthen your frame. You will be like a well-watered garden, like a spring whose waters never fail.

Your people will rebuild the ancient ruins and will raise up the age-old foundations; you will be called Repairer of Broken Walls, Restorer of Streets with Dwellings." – Isaiah 58:1-12 (NIV)

God takes note of our fasting. However, as we see in Isaiah 58, He also takes note of us and our conduct every day.

6. Capture Rhema Words and Visions

"My sheep listen to my voice; I know them, and they follow me." – John 10:27 (NIV)

God wants to speak to you. In fact, He may already be trying to speak to you, but you may not be sure how to listen and hear. As John 10:27 says, when we are one of His people, our inner spirit will know when it is Him talking. This is something I've had to learn.

I was not always able to hear God speaking to me. When I would hear someone else say, "and God told me..." it would make me upset that I wasn't hearing anything. "I want God to tell me things too," I would think, and I was serious about wanting that. The more I sought Him, the more experiences I started to have. At first, it started in dreams at night. Next, came times when He showed me things during prayer.

Let me back up a bit and say that God speaks to me during times when I am walking closely with Him and am ready to hear from Him. He has spoken to me (and may to you as well) in various ways including;

- dreams during the night,
- a word of encouragement or confirmation through another believer or situation,
- scriptures pertaining to my current situation at exactly the right moment,
- a vision, or picture in my mind during worship or prayer, or
- words directly spoken to my mind.

What do Rhema words mean?

Rhema is a Greek word that talks about an utterance or spoken message from the Lord. Logos is a Greek word that talks about the written Word of God. As an example, when we read the written (logos) Word, the Bible, God can speak a Rhema to our spirit and make a written passage come alive with special meaning for us. It also is when God speaks a specific, almost audible, message to your heart.

Whatever God speaks to you or shows you, be sure to write it down. So far, when God has spoken to me it hasn't usually been for casual conversation.

Every message has been an important revelation about who He sees me as, about His purposes, something I am to tell another person, something about a current situation, a lesson to be learned or correction, and/or about my future in Him.

7. Renew Your Mindset

It's time to identify and overcome your fears and the negative beliefs you have about yourself. As a man thinketh, so is he, right? *If you want what God wants for your life, you will need to think what God thinks about your life.* Anything less than having His perspective means you'll be missing out on something.

> If you want what God wants for your life, you will need to think what God thinks about your life.

The subconscious mind is much more powerful than most of us realize. Truth-be-told, our wrong mindsets put limitations on how God can work in, and through, our lives.

Visit chapters 12 and 13 for vital details about renewing your mindset.

I Need You, God

The inner work necessary to discover God's calling for you creates a relationship between you and God. In fact, the more you operate in your gifts and calling, the more deeply you'll realize you need God working in your life. My friend Dondi Scumaci, who is an author, speaker and business consultant, has a great personal story about needing more of Him.

Of this I am certain – I can do nothing apart from God and I can do amazing things with Him. Sometimes I am reminded of this in a gentle moment – a quiet reassurance that breaks through the noise and whispers encouragement. On other occasions I've been confronted head on (at the most inconvenient time).

I've learned (the hard way) that God won't be boxed in or conformed by formulas and techniques. He won't be manipulated by our schedules or spiritual rituals. A perfect example of falling into the "ritual" and losing the richness of God happened to me in front of 3,000 people. I still smile when I think of how inconvenient the timing was for this particular lesson.

For months I had been on a dead run. My life was marked by deadlines and plane flights. I was running on empty, physically, emotionally, and spiritually.

As was my habit, as I was being introduced to speak, I was praying for God's anointing on my message. At side stage I was saying all the "right" things.

"God bless this message and give me the words you would have me speak. Let your anointing fall on me now and give me wisdom." The answer was immediate and almost audible. If you'd been standing next to me just then, I think you might have heard, "My anointing does not fall on you Dondi– it clings to you when you spend time with me. You haven't been in my presence. You've been running on your power and strength. Go ahead and take this one on your own. I'll wait here."

This hit me just as I heard the announcement, "Please welcome Dondi Scumaci..." Oh Lord, No! Not now! I wanted to argue with God, but there was no time. I stepped onto that platform...alone.

Thankfully I did not fall flat on my face. God did not allow me to embarrass myself or disappoint the audience. It was fine, but it was not full. For me, the message was flat – a recitation, not a revelation. Others may not have noticed, but for me the difference was glaringly obvious.

I never want to perform like that again. I don't want to walk on the stage of life alone.

That night something important happened. The landscape of my life was split by a deep ravine. I became fully aware of my limitations. I no longer trusted myself and my natural abilities. At the same time, I had not learned to fully trust God – to rely completely on Him for every need and result. This gap created a huge canyon in my life. The distance from "here" to "there" was terrifying, but to fully experience my destiny I had to make that crossing.

The knowledge of my frailty wasn't designed to punish or expose me. It was offered to set me free – to lift the weight of the burden I had been carrying so long.

Perhaps I am still learning that lesson by degrees and inches. Learning to trust myself less and trust my God more. The ravine doesn't frighten me anymore – it calls me to cross and I reach for the hand of God to steady myself.

I appreciate Dondi's openness and willingness to share this story. I know we can all relate to periods of time where our relationship with God gets pushed to the side, and we try to work in our own strength. Even with the gifts He's given us, and work He's called us to, we are never meant to go it alone.

The inner work of seeking God and relying on Him is never finished. You can start today!

Summary

Through communication, a relationship with God can be formed. Through that relationship, God will speak to you about His call on your life. There are 7 spiritual realm, "inner work" ways for you to seek and connect with God:

1. Prayer and Meditation
2. Study the Bible
3. Worship and Praise
4. Find Biblically-Based Purpose, Vision and Calling Teaching
5. Fasting
6. Capture Rhema Words and Visions
7. Renew Your Mindset

Prayer: *Almighty God, thank You for allowing me to have direct access to You through prayer, reading Your Word, fasting, and worshipping You. I know You have a good plan for me. Please speak to my heart as I seek Your face through this inner work. I want to hear Your voice.*

Ask yourself:

- Which inner work areas am I already applying myself well in? In which do I need improvement?
- Is there someone who can be my accountability partner to keep me inspired to move forward?
- What can I do to experience more freedom in worship?
- What daily habits can I establish to pursue this inner work?

Affirmations:

My life is found within God's plan.
I am God's sheep, and I know His voice.
I keep my mind focused on God, and He leads me into all understanding.
I am becoming wise through spending time with the Lord.

Growth

"A man must know his destiny, and if he does not recognize it, he is lost. He must find out what fork in the road he should take, and if he has guts, he will take it." – George Patton

10.

How to Develop Your Gifts

It's time to learn and grow! But where and how, you ask?

The way in which you need to prepare yourself and develop your gifts will vary, depending on what your gifts are and how they're to be used. Having said that, no matter what gifts you have, some of the same ideas and learning strategies apply.

"If I had eight hours to chop down a tree, I'd spend six hours sharpening my ax." – Abraham Lincoln

Abraham Lincoln knew a secret. He knew how to ready himself; how to do what he needed to do, and do it well.

You've probably heard the saying that goes something like this: Anything not worth doing well isn't worth doing at all. That especially applies in the area of your gifts! Do you intend to discover your personal potential in life? When I think of people developing their gifts well and becoming skilled at using them, I believe it directly relates to personal potential. I like to use this equation:

Developing God-given gifts + Sharing them as God directs = Reaching one's full potential.

How many of you have ever watched the television show "American Idol?" As I'm writing this, there have been many successful TV seasons of this popular singing talent show. Thousands of wanna-be singing stars gather at the American Idol try-out sites across the country. Out of these thousands of hopefuls, a handful of show winners have gone on to be famous singers with recording contracts and millions of adoring fans.

"For many are called, but few are chosen." – Matthew 22:14 (NLT)

American Idol producers send a nationwide call for try-outs to everyone that fits the contest requirements. Only several thousand people show up. Where are the other millions that are interested in this process? Sitting and watching from the comfort of their armchairs. Even within this try-out group of thousands, only several dozen are chosen to move on and be on each show.

The same happens with God. He calls all men to Himself, from all countries, races and peoples. A certain segment of the population trusts in His name. Again, even this segment of believers will be called and tested further, and a few of these will show up and be chosen. God will show Himself strong through this few.

The people who are chosen for American Idol are serious about singing. None of the silly, bad singer folks get chosen, as they are not qualified. Why aren't they qualified? They haven't developed their gifts. They may not even actually have that gift at all, but wish they did.

The chosen few have aligned their actions and intentions to pursue their passion of singing. They have a gift, they've embraced it and are actively developing it.

God is looking for people who are aware of what He's placed in them, and recognize His call. Just like those who are selected to be on American Idol, people in this select group bring their gifts forth (of whatever kind it might be) with courage. Not only have they chosen to boldly share it with others, but first have gone the extra mile to develop it and become skilled.

Progression:

- ✓ Gift is identified
- ✓ Gift is acknowledged and cherished
- ✓ Gift is developed and honed
- ✓ Gift becomes a skill
- ✓ Gift can be boldly shared

My desire for you is to be one of the people who step out in excellence. It will require something of you though. Anytime you want to grow, in any area of life, something will be required. The Bible says to count the cost before you begin a work. Expect growth to cost you time, effort and probably money. It is well worth it!

"Pour your purse into your head." – Benjamin Franklin

Did you know that it's okay to spend money on the process of personal and spiritual growth? Get rid of the mindset that says spending money on personal and spiritual growth is a waste. That is simply not true. In Proverbs, we are advised that although it may cost us all we have, God directs us to get wisdom and understanding. Apparently, getting wisdom has the highest return on investment (ROI)!

I have a special friend named Noreen Jacks. Noreen and I partner in several ways, including leading www.TheWallofPrayer.com, and she's also an accomplished Bible teacher and author. She's taken the time to seek God about His calling for her and to seek growth and gift development. She is someone who's really stepped out into her calling. Here is a snapshot of her journey:

More than three decades of Bible teaching began with a simple invitation from a neighbor, asking me to teach a weekly religious education class to second graders at our local church. As a newlywed, teaching was the last thing on my mind. I had no background or interest in teaching, and my primary concern was having a baby.

To say I was depressed at that time in my life would be an understatement. Having recently suffered a miscarriage early in my first pregnancy, I wondered if I would ever hear the pitter-patter of little feet scampering around my home. Self-absorbed in misery, I attempted to put the second grade class out of my mind, but I could not shake the stirring conviction of the Holy Spirit that came upon me.

I eventually consented to teach the class, but not without first making a deal with God. Such unholy boldness! I told the Lord I would answer His call if He would give me the desires of my heart; the baby I longed to nurture. In faith, I kept my end of the bargain and began my new adventure.

Within a few short weeks after beginning my teaching assignment, the Lord answered my prayers. I was joyfully pregnant again! In God's appointed time, I gave birth to the first of four sons, all of whom were as lively as my little second graders. God has many ways of preparing His people for ministry.

When I said "yes" to the Lord concerning my initial teaching assignment, I was unaware that He was calling me to a lifetime of service to Him. Shortly afterward, I organized a neighborhood Bible Study that met in my home and in the park for several years, until my pastor's wife invited me to bring the group to church. I have been teaching many of the same ladies every Tuesday morning for twenty-three years. A few of the ladies have been together for over forty years. God is so good!

Not only has the Lord provided many teaching opportunities for me through the years in places like the county jail and women's retreats, He has also blessed me with a wonderful Bible college education, for which I am most grateful. Only God could have taken a bored student from junior college dropout status to a doctoral degree in Biblical Studies and Theology. He truly helped me to discover my hidden gifts and potential.

By God's grace, I have had the privilege of leading tours to the Holy Land, publishing books, sharing at various churches, conferences, and more recently, teaching on God's Learning Channel, an international Christian television network. All of these blessings came to pass because I said "yes" to teaching God's little ones about His glory and grace. I pray that you will also allow the Lord to stir up the gifts that are within you.

As you can see, Noreen's calling was found in a "small beginning." With God's help, she took that small beginning and ran with it. Along the way, she pushed out of her comfort zones and found the education and learning opportunities she needed to be more effective. As a result of her growth and obedience, you can see how mightily God uses her now for His purposes.

Just as with a career or hobby, you'll want to improve, acquire more knowledge, build practical skills and learn to use your gifts effectively. We do this through getting knowledge, understanding and wisdom.

Knowledge, understanding and wisdom show a progression of competency:

1. Knowledge – The facts, awareness and information you attain. When you first realized God gives each person gifts, you received new knowledge.

2. Understanding – When you discovered your gifts, you gained new understanding about yourself and God's plan for you.

3. Wisdom – Confidence in Godly principles, paired with effective actions, creates wisdom. When you figure out how to follow God's will for sharing your gifts, then step out and share them, that action shows evidence of growing in wisdom.

"The fear of the LORD is the beginning of wisdom, and knowledge of the Holy One is understanding." – Proverbs 9:10 (NIV)

Using that progression, step one for you will be collecting knowledge. Where can knowledge be collected? That depends on what kind you need. The first obvious place to look is in the Bible. Chances are, in the Bible there is someone who had a gift like yours. Learn from their example.

If your calling involves leading a group of people or a cause, study biblical leaders. If your calling involves being in business, do a study on all the business people and principles found in the Bible. If writing and teaching is part of your calling, use the scriptures as an amazing example of storytelling and teaching styles. In a nutshell, the Bible is a boundless source to learn from.

Official schooling and higher education may be necessary, depending on your calling and how your gifts need to be developed.

• Is there a class available either online or in your community where you can learn?
• Should you attain a certain certification, license or degree for your field of work?
• Apprenticeship or vocational education may be appropriate for developing your gifts.

Special Note: Your degree, certification, licensing, etc., may qualify you for a job or position. However, *only God qualifies you to operate in your calling.* But, honing your skills through learning opportunities will make you a more effective tool in God's hands.

> Only God qualifies you to operate in your calling.

Another traditional way to learn is by finding appropriate training.

- Does your church offer a mentor, training program, team, or class for your type of gift?
- As we've discussed, find trustworthy mentors who teach you individually.
- The internet is a vast resource for ideas, training and learning opportunities.
- Can you purchase CD's or DVD's from trusted sources with the teachings you need?
- Are there specific books to read on your topic of need?
- Does your field have associations or chapters you could join?
- Can you attend camps, coaching sessions or retreats for further training?

A great way to learn is by observing or serving with others who have similar giftings.

Who is in your community, family, church, network, or workplace that you could learn from? You won't always have direct access to those you'd like to learn from, but indirect learning is still extremely helpful. I've learned a great deal by observing and serving with others. I've learned what works well, what I would do differently and how to not re-invent the wheel. Even people who you don't know personally, but respect, can be observed. For example:

- Other business people, via their online videos, interviews, their courses of action, books they've written, or leadership style.
- Other writers, by reading their work, reading interviews they do, understanding their methods or writing habits, etc.
- Other speakers, through listening to their speeches, evaluating their structure and the effect it has on audiences.
- Other ministers, as they speak, teach, write and present on TV, radio, in local churches, on blogs, etc.

- Other artists, by studying their work, systems and methods.
- Other medical care professionals by volunteering at hospitals or care homes, or by reading their reports in medical journals.

It's easy, because you do not need to ask for their spare time or need their permission!

I don't think any of us are ever completely done collecting knowledge. However, I know it's tempting to hang out in the knowledge-collecting phase for a while (or forever). Don't stop there for too long and become a perpetual student who never actually steps out. Move on to step two, which is gaining understanding.

Now that you've built some knowledge through studying scripture, training, classes, and observing others, you can do some practicing. Practice will help you to gain understanding.

Ideas for practicing with your gifts to gain more understanding:

- Churches and ministries usually offer a great environment to practice using your gifts.
- Classroom and training situations are great places to practice since they may require assignments, role play and practical application.
- Look for any opportunities at home, work, or in the community to put into practice what you've learned.
- Step out in small ways at first, and get feedback from trusted sources.
- Practice – re-adjust – repeat!

When I was on a quest to gain public speaking skills, I did (and still do) several things including;

- observing examples of other speakers,
- reading speaking tips and strategies online,
- listening to teleseminars (phone trainings given by experts) on the topic,
- took a personal inventory and evaluated my own skill level,
- practiced talking out loud while alone,
- found opportunities to speak and present for small groups,
- joined a speaking club, and
- took a public speaking class every week for 7 months.

Using my public speaking example, I gained knowledge by reading about good speaking tips, evaluating my own skills and listening to other speakers and instructors. Next, I gained understanding through practicing in front of classmates and instructors. I not only had the opportunities to practice, but I also received feedback, help and encouragement. I put myself in a vulnerable position to mold my abilities. All of this work helped my mind and mouth understand how to be effective at speaking and presenting in front of others.

Partially, this understanding step involves developing character, being teachable and renewing your mind as well. Your mindsets become renewed about who you see yourself as. Of course, God already knows what you are capable of, but sometimes it may take your mindset and self-image a while to catch up!

And now, let's move on to wisdom. The Bible says that God freely gives wisdom to all who ask. For our discussion here, my definition of *wisdom is combining God's will with your knowledge and understanding, your gifts, and spiritual discernment, and then taking effective action.* It's having the practical skills *and* the spiritual understanding, then going out into the world and doing "it," whatever "it" is. Without action or expression, wisdom is not proven. Wisdom must be demonstrated if it's to have any value.

> Wisdom is combining God's will with your knowledge and understanding, your gifts, and spiritual discernment, and then taking effective action.

God wants to use anyone willing, but how much more does He want to use a willing skilled person! Prepare yourself for your special work as well as you possibly can. Be ready to be a specialized tool in the Master's hands.

> *"'Yes,' the king replied, 'and to those who use well what they are given, even more will be given. But from those who do nothing, even what little they have will be taken away.'"* – Luke 19:26 (NLT)

Summary

Developing your gifts is a must, and there are potentially many ways to do so. It's going to cost you something, yet the cost is worthwhile.

Getting knowledge, understanding and wisdom shows a progression of competency. Getting knowledge means acquiring facts and information. Understanding comes when you start to work with the information you've acquired, and get an image of how to use it. Wisdom is the combination of knowledge, spiritual discernment and practical action. God desires to give you wisdom, and wants you to seek it out.

Depending on what you need to learn, traditional higher education, training programs or sessions, observing others and/or studying the scriptures may fit your needs. God desires for us to be skilled instruments in His hand by honing our gifts and operating in excellence.

Prayer: *Thank You God – You are so good! You know exactly who I need to connect with and learn from. Help me to gain knowledge, understanding and wisdom in the area of my gifts and calling Lord. Finish the work You have started in me. Provide me with the finances needed and/or the free opportunities to get wisdom. Show me favor Lord as I develop the gifts You have given me. You are orchestrating the plan now, and I thank You.*

Ask yourself:

- Who can I learn from?
- Am I willing to take the time and do the hard work of developing my gifts?
- What opportunities to develop my gifts are available to me now?

Affirmations:

I don't need to have all the answers.
I seek wise counsel by allowing mature, wise people to mentor me.
God gives me the connections and learning opportunities that I need.
The more I grow, the better my impact becomes.
I do what I do, well.

11.
Visionary Goal Setting

"Write the vision and make it plain on tablets, that he may run who reads it." – Habakkuk 2:2 (NKJV)

"Without goals, resources and dreams are dissipated." – Pastor Ray Frederick

Ready, Set...Goals!

As you work on developing your gifts and getting ready to step out into your calling, setting goals will be very helpful. After all, did you know that God has plans and goals? Yes, He is a visionary goal-setter. To be a visionary goal-setter means to be creative, far-seeing, prophetic and to do something new.

Since your gifts and calling are meant to help others in some meaningful way, what is your plan to make that happen? Now is the time to make a plan and get clarity on God's next steps for you and your gifts.

Look at these two words:

Planning
Planting

Notice what they both have in common? A plan.

Some of us don't like setting goals or planning, but when you plan for your future, you plant for your future. A wise person once told me, "Sow where you want to go." Sowing literally means to plant seeds into soil. In this case, you are sowing (planning) where God wants you to go with your gifts.

When I think of the word "plant," to me it involves action and indicates intentional forethought about the future harvest. That's exactly your phase right now – you're planting things into your heart, mind and spirit that will set a course for a harvest of some kind.

How Do I Set Goals?

Now that you see *why* it's important to set goals, let's talk about *how* to set them. These five goal setting tips can be applied to any area of life, including setting goals for spiritual growth and using your gifts.

1. Write goals on paper

In Habakkuk 2, it says to write the vision and make it plain, meaning make them clear and concise. Put them somewhere you can see them often. If the goals contained in your head do not make it out, they turn into wishes or daydreams. If you have goals that aren't written down, the likelihood is that you aren't serious about them and they won't materialize.

I recommend keeping a goals journal or notebook. I have a "faith board" next to my nightstand, which is also a fun idea.

2. Let others know about your goals

The second half of Habakkuk 2:2 talks about other people running with the vision too. Why do you think it says that? Here's what I think: The vision the Lord gives you almost always involves or requires support from others. Tell other people about your goals so you can get help *and* accountability partners at the same time.

3. Start with the end in mind

What is your end goal? My goals mentor, Pastor Ray Frederick, gave me this advice one day: "*Goal setting will force you to enter a process to figure out what it is that you want.*" Many of us easily set short term goals because we have a clear vision for our upcoming week or month. Unfortunately, most of us don't have a vision for our lives, work and service 10-20 years from now.

Imagine it's the last day of your life on earth, decades from now. What is it that you've accomplished? What valuable work have you been involved in? What kind of positive impact have you made?

This is where your knowledge of God's calling comes in. Once you understand the mission He has for you, it's much easier to clarify your life goals. When you figure that out, when you catch the vision for hearing "well done good and faithful servant" at the end of your life, then you can work your way backwards to determine what the interim steps, goals and actions need to be.

4. Make goals measureable and attainable

By making goals measurable, they become much more specific. You make them measurable by including parameters like timeframes, quantities and dollar amounts (as are applicable to the goal type).

For example, which goal is more specific, because it is measurable?

1. Further my education.
2. Complete my four-year degree through an online college within the next two years.

Number two, of course, is more specific. Can you see how the specifics included in goal number two makes it clearer to your mind and therefore more attainable? Goal number one is very vague. Will it ever actually happen? Maybe, but most likely not. Goal number two has it all - the what, where, when, and how.

Along with creating "attainable" goals, set goals that challenge you but aren't so far-fetched that there's no possible way they can be reached. Unrealistic goals are discouraging! However, there is one exception: If God tells or shows you it will happen. In that case, it's a promise directly from the Lord. Even if it seems unrealistic to others, it will come to pass in partnership with your belief and obedience.

5. Let God shape your goals

Once again, you know that God is in control, right? As His people, opening up this planning phase to Him is prudent. Not doing so would be absurd! He already knows what you need to do and what goals are needed to get there. Just ask, and then wait for His answers!

> *"In his heart a man plans his course, but the LORD determines his steps."* – Proverbs 16:9 (NIV)

Planning is good. Even though God has the final say, please don't believe that planning and setting goals isn't necessary – it is. Your task is to create God-directed goals and plans. God *will* work with that.

The Role of Emotion

Once your goals are set, there's one more ingredient you need to cement them in: E*motion. Without an emotional attachment to a goal, you won't care about achieving it.* Although I know that unchecked emotions can be like a car driving into a ditch and getting stuck, even so, you need emotions with goals. Without an emotion attached, a vision for your future doesn't become real.

> Without an emotional attachment to a goal, you won't care about achieving it.

I used to devalue emotions, but now I understand more about how to use them. Think about these statements:

- You cannot connect to God or with God without your heart and emotions involved.
- You cannot connect to His calling for you, goals, vision, dreams, etc., without your emotions being invested in them.
- God's promises, Word and calling for you cannot stay head knowledge, because you won't believe in them.

Plainly said, goals without a corresponding emotion are worthless. Just as Habakkuk 2:2 says to write the vision down, they also need to be written on your heart.

How can you attach emotion to your goals? Here are a few ideas:

- Through prayer and meditation, basing goals on what's already a heart's desire
- Visualizing them being completed, and experiencing how that would feel
- By connecting them with music on a visual slideshow

Why does someone change their diet and lose weight? Because they got scared, remorseful or nervous (emotions) when the doctor gave them serious news about their reduced life expectancy.

Why would a person step out and volunteer at a non-profit organization's event? Because their emotions were touched when they saw a video showing the great need of the people this organization serves.

If your goal is to discover God's calling for your life, get your emotions involved. Just like believing in a promise, the head knowledge or goal item needs to move from your logical mind and be planted in your heart. From there, it gets its strength to endure.

Your Brain Likes Goals

I've learned interesting information from brain experts and psychologists about the correlation between our brains and our goals, visualization, achievement, and self-image. One interesting fact is that our brains have a goal-seeking mechanism inside called the Reticular Activating System (RAS).

Have you noticed that when you're stuck in an undecided frame of mind, things seem foggy, confusing and scattered? Without a clear image of a goal, actually being visualized in your brain, your RAS will not get going. It wants to make plans to achieve goals; goals that are defined and decided upon.

Several years ago, my brother-in-law was contemplating moving back to our area. For about twelve months he contemplated it. Undecided and unresolved, the issue caused him to feel unsettled and frustrated. Finally, one day, he made the decision in an instant. Immediately, his disposition changed and he started creating plans to make the move. He set a move date, and the flurry of action necessary to cover all the details began. It was like someone switched on a lighted path.

Your brain likes to have a clear goal. Once you give it one, once you make a decision, it starts to work out a plan of action and the steps needed to reach it. Additionally, your brain wants to be able to visualize the goal already completed and for your self-image to agree that it can be achieved.

That is important! If you cannot visualize it ("see it"), then your brain can't make a plan to get there. If your self-image says you cannot do something, or should not have something, there will be emotional and logical conflict and your RAS will not activate.

Again, we see how believing in God's plan for our life is so essential. Where there is no vision, truly being able to see it taking place, the people perish.

So if you aren't planning to succeed, what are you planning to do?

> So if you aren't planning to succeed, what are you planning to do?

Summary

God has plans and goals, and we are wise to have them too. Planning can be compared to planting, and putting intentional forethought into our future harvest.

There are five important aspects of setting goals, which are:

1. Write goals on paper
2. Let others know about your goals
3. Start with the end in mind
4. Make goals measurable and attainable
5. Let God shape your goals

When you set goals, each goal needs to have an emotion attached to it. Without moving goals from your logical mind to your heart (where emotions live), you'll be detached from the outcome of your goal. Goals without a corresponding emotion are worthless, so write them on your heart.

Your self-image, your brain, the vision God gives you for your future, and decision-making all play a part in goal-setting. The clearer your vision is, and the more detailed your goals are, the more likely it is that you can achieve them.

Prayer: *Father God, Your will be done on earth as it is in Heaven. Your will be done in my life and heart. Today, help me to plan for the good future you are preparing. Lead me down the right path, and help me make the right decisions. Guide my mind to set goals that You will establish. Help me to be dedicated to this journey with You.*

Ask yourself:

- Am I planning to succeed? In what ways?
- What are my goals? Do I have them written down?
- When I have goals set, am I open to allowing God to change them?

Affirmations:

I write down goals and vision, and get clarity from the Lord.
I plan ahead for a successful harvest.
My plans and goals are flexible, as God continues to show me more about my calling.

12.

Renew Your Mindset

Change your mind. *It's one thing to know what God's plan is for your life, and it's another to believe in your capacity to step out into it.* Your mind will not move forward with something it does not believe. To believe something, it not only must be understood in our minds, but also understood within our hearts. Believing grows from our heads to our hearts and then also lives within our emotions.

> It's one thing to know what God's plan is for your life, and it's another to believe in your capacity to step out into it.

"Do not conform any longer to the pattern of this world, but be transformed by the renewing of your mind." – Romans 12:2a (NIV)

Change starts in our minds, moves to our hearts and then becomes an outward expression. Are you ready to change your mind so you can get a new image of you; an image of being used by God and operating in your calling? He wants to use you for a special purpose, but first He must speak words of life to your spirit to empower you with hope, courage, strength and faith.

I've had to do massive amounts of mindset renewal work. If it were possible, listening to recordings of my thoughts from 20, 15, 10, 5, or even 2 years ago would be very eye-opening! I used to see myself as small, timid, gifted yet restricted, inhibited, scattered, and just average. I didn't believe God could use me to do anything important and had no vision for myself as a leader - not in the least. God had to remove certain things from my mindset and replace them with His truth.

Too many of us have been shaped and conformed to the world and its expectations, values and appearance. Some of us have been negatively shaped by bad past experiences and trauma. Some of us believe harmful messages we've been fed. When this happens, finding the pure, simple, God-shaped image of who we really are is difficult because of the thick "world crust" that has formed on the outside.

Peel away the layers of who the world expects you to be; the fears, failures, hurts, and images of how you should look, what you should want, and what you should think. You may even need to "throw off" your successes and pride before you can find the beautiful core of who you are. How, you ask? That answer may be slightly different for each individual, but it all starts with renewing your mind.

Typically, these are the main areas of mindset renewal that many of us struggle with:

- Trust
- Self-Image
- Hope and Faith
- Spoken Words
- Kicking Fear Out

Trust

Let me ask you this: Do you trust God, even if you don't trust yourself? Do you trust that when God calls you to step out, that He knows what He's doing?

In God's mind, it's an easy decision from His perspective. He says, "Simply step, and I will supply." From our perspective, it's often a bit more complicated than that - or so we think!

> *"Be confident, my heart, because the Lord has been good to me."* – Psalm 116:7 (TEV)

When children are young, many simple tasks are difficult for small hands. The exclamation (or whine), "I can't do it!" can be heard time and again at the first sign of difficulty.

For example, my young daughter used to become very frustrated by little things like snapping coats closed, opening lids or clicking the seatbelts in. Often, my challenging answer to her was, "I know it's hard. Are you going to give up?" To her credit, she almost always said, "No." I admire that in her!

When these situations came up with my daughter, I knew she could do it. It wasn't a matter of ability; it was a lack of persistence, or a throw-in-the-towel issue. When it was something that I knew was beyond her capacity,

I stepped in to help as soon as possible. When she accomplished something difficult, it boosted her confidence. She learned to persevere and overcome. I sense that God may observe us and see how we handle adversity at times too, just like this.

In the same way, God knows what we are capable of better than we do. When He says, "Move forward," should we stay standing still? When He says, "I Am All-Sufficient," do we believe that? Will we trust in His ability to fill in our gaps when we think we're not ready?

As Joyce Meyer would say, "Sometimes, we just have to do it afraid."

Have you ever watched the classic Christmas movie *It's a Wonderful Life*? That movie really speaks to me, in many ways, but specifically about trust in God's plan. The main character, George Bailey, took over his small town's building and loan business that his father had started. God put a deep desire in George's heart to make a big difference in the world and to put people first. Unfortunately, in George's mind, that meant dreams and plans of travel and big, grandiose projects. When that plan was not realized, it caused George to live a frustrated life. He became weary in doing good, and felt stuck in his little hometown.

When George Bailey is at the end of his rope, when he's experienced a life full of frustration, yet full and rich with blessings (love, relationships, purpose, generosity, provision, etc.), God sends an angel to show him what his community and loved ones' lives would have been like without him. George finally understands how extremely valuable his daily actions, decisions and life have been. The impact he made in his community was life changing.

God did have plans for George to make a big difference in the world. At the end, George saw how God had orchestrated it all along. George simply needed to accept his assignment. Once he did, he immediately understood his special place in God's plan and was content.

The movie made me ask this question, "Will I trust and agree with God's plan or cling to my own expectations of what it should 'look' like?" Once God shows you His will and plan for your life, will *you* trust and agree with it? Will you trust that if He calls, and you know without a doubt that it's His will, that He is with you?

Self-Image

What you believe about yourself is imperative to your success. God wants to change your self-image to match His image of who you are. Who your self-image says you are, is most likely not how God fully sees you.

> What you believe about yourself is imperative to your success.

Do you struggle with a poor self-image? People who struggle with a negative self-image have limiting beliefs about themselves. Limiting beliefs are just what they sound like; beliefs, or false-truths we cling to that put parameters and limitations on what we expect from ourselves and for our future. They also limit what God can do in our lives.

> *"And he [Jesus] did not do many miracles there because of their lack of faith."* – Matthew 13:58 (NIV)

Please don't put limitations on what God can do in your life because of limiting beliefs you have about yourself! These next examples show words and thoughts that people say or think that stem from limiting beliefs:

- My past failure and shame disqualify me from serving God now.
- I cannot have what those other people have.
- When I'm old, I expect that I will be lonely and feeble.
- I could never do that.
- I will hate every job that I have, and will be working only for the money.
- My current state of existence is as good as it gets.
- I was victimized and will continue to be victimized by others, and I can't do anything about it.
- My gifts aren't very valuable.
- I am worthless and my opinions don't matter.

Examples of limiting beliefs that people carry around within themselves could fill dozens of pages! Pay attention to your thoughts that say, "I can't...," that resist change or have a negative outlook on something. Thoughts like these damage our true potential, and possibly even the potential of those around us.

Have you noticed in the Bible that God Himself spoke to nearly every person He wanted to use for His purposes, to change their self-image? Yes. Think about it; Abraham, Sarah, Hagar, Jacob, Moses, Aaron, Joshua, Gideon, Jeremiah, David, Samuel, Mary, Paul, Peter, and many others needed a revelation about what they were capable of. And not only of what they were capable of, but also a revelation of who they were born to be and their part in God's plan. God had to change their minds.

At age 99, with no legitimate children, Abraham had this encounter with God (from Genesis 17 - NIV):

"Abram fell facedown, and God said to him, "As for me, this is my covenant with you: You will be the father of many nations. No longer will you be called Abram; your name will be Abraham, for I have made you a father of many nations. I will make you very fruitful; I will make nations of you, and kings will come from you. I will establish my covenant as an everlasting covenant between me and you and your descendants after you for the generations to come, to be your God and the God of your descendants after you."

Wow – that is definitely a life-changing, self-image changing discussion. God even changed his identity by giving him a new name, and then He changed Abraham's wife's name too!

Here is another example of God's intervention with Gideon in the Old Testament book of Judges, chapter 6 (NIV):

"When the angel of the LORD appeared to Gideon, he said, "The LORD is with you, mighty warrior."
"Pardon me, my lord," Gideon replied, "but if the LORD is with us, why has all this happened to us? Where are all his wonders that our ancestors told us about when they said, 'Did not the LORD bring us up out of Egypt?' But now the LORD has abandoned us and given us into the hand of Midian."
The LORD turned to him and said, "Go in the strength you have and save Israel out of Midian's hand. Am I not sending you?"
"Pardon me, my lord," Gideon replied, "but how can I save Israel? My clan is the weakest in Manasseh, and I am the least in my family."

I identify with Gideon's feelings of weakness and insignificance. "What can I do? Do you know who you're talking to God? Me, a mighty warrior? What? I'm a nobody." Maybe you can relate too. Nonetheless, do you know that Gideon went on to do mighty, courageous things? Yes! At first, he obeyed God's commands nervously, secretly. Then, as he trusted the Lord more, he did so boldly.

It's time for a new revelation. God wants to give you authority in some area; in some kind of message that He wants to convey to people. Maybe it's His message of hope, healing, forgiveness, repentance, purity, worship, courage, grace, freedom, mercy, recovery, mentoring, building up, truth, wisdom, battle, or love, etc. He has a place established for you. If you want to step out into it, it's time to get past inadequate feelings, a small or negative self-image and past failures. You are who God says you are, *not* what a negative self-image says that you are.

Lay down your limiting beliefs and negative self-image. If God calls you to it, He will be with you through it. If you look at your own limited resources, limited wisdom and knowledge, limited finances, limited skills, etc., it will seem like you are not enough to complete the task asked of you. Guess what - you *aren't* enough. *But,* God with you is exceedingly more than enough. Praise the Lord! That is good news...

Hope and Faith

What do you see for your future? Hope and faith are all about "seeing" something that does not exist yet in the natural realm. They're about believing a promise or having a vision from God for your future, then waiting for it to come to pass.

> *"Now faith is the substance of things hoped for, the evidence of things not seen."* – Hebrews 11:1 (KJV)

Think of it like farming. Imagine this scene in your mind:

You are a farmer with ten acres of farmland. Your house is on the first acre, near the road, and then behind that is nine full acres of garden. Right now, the garden needs much preparation; weeds, rocks, grass, sticks, and vines have taken over. After weeks of removing the old gunk, turning the soil and adding fertilizer, you look out from your porch and see the rich, dark soil ready for seeds. Seeding takes time, and you have to have a sound plan and the right tools to ensure a good harvest.

You push seed after seed into the ground, carefully aligning each row. Finally, seeding is complete. You take your position in the rocking chair on the porch and wait. Much effort and work is done, for now. Although there is zero evidence that anything is happening, you have hope for your coming harvest. Each day you water, and wait. Water and wait. You have faith that your good effort will establish something tangible. You still see nothing visible.

"For we live by faith, not by sight." – 2 Corinthians 5:7 (NIV)

A couple weeks later, you wake up, and go out to the porch as usual. You see signs of life! Small, green shoots have come up sporadically. It's very exciting! About a week after that, you survey the full nine acres and see that it's completely covered in fresh, green plants bursting up everywhere. Something big is on the way. Are you ready?

As we know through the Bible, our life in the spiritual realm matches this natural process. When it comes to having hope and faith about God's plan for your life, here are a few thoughts to consider:

- You have soil to tend; it's your heart and mind. Real things grow there, starting as thoughts at first, and then they become tangible things, like decisions, words and actions.
- Too often we try to plant something new before we prepare our soil. Get rid of the old gunk (bad habits, negative actions and emotions, unhealthy relationships, etc.) and turn the soil (renew our minds) and add fertilizer (new wisdom) first.
- Leaving a cleaned-up field idle invites the weeds to grow again. Weeds need no invitation; they are the default crop. Quickly replace the gunk with intentionally planted seeds. Be purposeful about what you plant in your heart's soil.
- *Waiting takes great faith. Don't walk away from your field prematurely.*
- Seeing the signs of life is physical evidence of things hoped for, but is not time for slacking off.
- Seeing a huge, coming harvest can be intimidating. Plan ahead for an overflow of blessing so that you are ready to receive it.
- Good stewardship in small things qualifies you for more. Increase your capacity.
- Be intentional about what happens in your fields; relationship fields, business fields,

> Waiting takes great faith. Don't walk away from your field prematurely.

spiritual fields, physical health fields, etc. Plant, tend and harvest with purpose and faith.

I'm not going to lie or put rose colored glasses on when I talk about this. Having hope and faith in things that are not seen can be very difficult in our world. Think about this question: Is it easier to have faith and an expectation for bad things to happen in your life or for good things?

Unfortunately, it's really easy to believe that bad things will come. Why is that easier than believing for blessings and good? Because it goes against this world's default system, and often we see so much negative happening around us that it's easy to expect it for ourselves as well. Believing for blessings, positive outcomes, healing, miracles, safety, etc., goes against the grain of our fallen world.

However, you as God's child, live in God's Kingdom system. Because of that, He asks you to have faith and lasting hope for the things He promises and speaks to you about. Having hope and faith in the things of God requires an intentional changing of your mindset. Each day, as you renew your mind, be purposeful about holding on to hope and faith. If you aren't, it will dwindle, and the weeds will start to grow again.

God has plans for you. Maybe by now He's spoken to you about them or shown you something about your future and calling. Sometimes you'll have to wait for it. We might be tempted to force our promise from God to happen in our timeframe, or make up our own way to manifest it. Genesis chapter 15 (NIV) includes a great example of a family who got tired of waiting, and came up with their own plan for getting God's promise. Here was God's promise to them:

"After this, the word of the LORD came to Abram in a vision: "Do not be afraid, Abram. I am your shield, your very great reward."

But Abram said, "Sovereign LORD, what can you give me since I remain childless and the one who will inherit my estate is Eliezer of Damascus?" And Abram said, "You have given me no children; so a servant in my household will be my heir."

Then the word of the LORD came to him: "This man will not be your heir, but a son who is your own flesh and blood will be your heir." He took him outside and said, "Look up at the sky and count the stars—if indeed you can count them." Then he said to him, "So shall your offspring be."

Abram believed the LORD, and he credited it to him as righteousness."

Shortly after this encounter with the Lord, Abram (later to become Abraham) had a different encounter. Unfortunately, it was not an encounter that God was directing him to have. In fact, it ended up being a huge source of strife in his family. To me, it looked like Sarai and Abram were trying to speed up the process of getting God's promise. Here's the next set of events found in Genesis chapter 16 (NIV):

Now Sarai, Abram's wife, had borne him no children. But she had an Egyptian slave named Hagar; so she said to Abram, "The LORD has kept me from having children. Go, sleep with my slave; perhaps I can build a family through her."

Abram agreed to what Sarai said. So after Abram had been living in Canaan ten years, Sarai his wife took her Egyptian slave Hagar and gave her to her husband to be his wife. He slept with Hagar, and she conceived.

When she knew she was pregnant, she began to despise her mistress. Then Sarai said to Abram, "You are responsible for the wrong I am suffering. I put my slave in your arms, and now that she knows she is pregnant, she despises me. May the LORD judge between you and me."

"Your slave is in your hands," Abram said. "Do with her whatever you think best." Then Sarai mistreated Hagar; so she fled from her.

The angel of the LORD found Hagar near a spring in the desert; it was the spring that is beside the road to Shur. And he said, "Hagar, slave of Sarai, where have you come from, and where are you going?"

"I'm running away from my mistress Sarai," she answered.

Then the angel of the LORD told her, "Go back to your mistress and submit to her." The angel added, "I will increase your descendants so much that they will be too numerous to count."

The angel of the LORD also said to her: "You are now pregnant and you will give birth to a son. You shall name him Ishmael, for the LORD has heard of your misery. He will be a wild donkey of a man; his hand will be against everyone and everyone's hand against him, and he will live in hostility toward all his brothers."

In this Genesis story of Sarai (Sarah), Abram (Abraham) and Hagar, it becomes obvious that our desires to see God's plan come to pass could cause us to short-cut God's route. Even so, notice that God's plan still prevailed. Hope and faith often also requires patience. I can see myself falling into this trap if I'm not careful, so this situation is a great reminder seek God's plan and God's timing!

*"And without faith it is impossible to please God, because
anyone who comes to him must believe that he exists and
that he rewards those who earnestly seek him.*

*By faith Noah, when warned about things not yet seen,
in holy fear built an ark to save his family. By his faith he
condemned the world and became heir of the righteousness
that is in keeping with faith."* – Hebrews 11:6-7 (NIV)

Your faith and hope pleases God. He puts an extremely high value on faith. In fact, in Luke 18:8 (NIV), Jesus asked this question: *"...when the Son of Man comes, will He find faith on the earth?"* God has a lot to teach us about having strong faith. Testing it makes it stronger! Know that God is always faithful to you; it's part of His character, and He also wants it to become part of yours.

Spoken Words

*"May these words of my mouth and this meditation of my heart be pleasing
in your sight, LORD, my Rock and my Redeemer."* – Psalm 19:14 (NIV)

*"The soothing tongue is a tree of life, but a perverse tongue
crushes the spirit."* – Proverbs 15:4 (NIV)

Do you want to see good days and love your life? I sure do! In 1 Peter 3:10 (NIV), Peter writes to believers about their words saying, *"Whoever would love life and see good days must keep their tongue from evil and their lips from deceitful speech."* That's a serious cautioning!

It's time to say something – something that will support and promote the kind of future God wants for you. Did you know that your words, the actual words that come out of your mouth, are a creative force? Yes they are. Do you know why? God's words are a creative force and you are made in His image, in His likeness.

It's time to speak, in faith, some things into existence. As His child, you have promises from God. He has already established certain things in the spirit realm and you haven't seen them show up yet. You may just need to ask. Or, it may be a bigger issue related to the words that come out (or don't come out) of your mouth.

My good friend, Tammy Redmon, is one of the best people I know to discuss this topic. She's passionate about teaching people to not remain victims of their negative self-talk and haphazard spoken words. As the co-founders of Koinonia Business Women, she and I have had many conversations on the topic of mindset. When we're at meetings or talking with business women, Tammy is keenly aware of the words people use about their past, current situations, future and potential.

She notices people all the time speaking discouraging words about themselves; knowing that those words stem from a negative mindset or limiting belief. She is compelled to help them "re-frame" their perspectives because words are so powerful. That is why I lovingly call her "The Word Cop!"

Here's what she has to say to you:

Looking back to the beginning of the world, everything that God created was spoken into being. In fact, in Genesis 1, He spoke 9 times for things to "be." The glorious thing is that we have that very same power in our own lives; to speak creation!

We have been given authority over every living thing; we have that power through our spoken words.

The power of the spoken word also shows up when Jesus was confronted by the Devil in Matthew 4:1-11. "Since you are God's Son, speak the word that will turn these stones into loaves of bread." Jesus replied quoting Deuteronomy: "It takes more than bread to stay alive. It takes a steady stream of words from God's mouth."

Even the Devil knows the power of our words! And what I love about this section of scripture is that Jesus rebuked the Devil three times with the authority of his Word!

Let's remember we have the full authority operating in and through us; that very same power of the tongue, to use it to edify and lift up, make our confessions known to God, tear down and wipe out our enemy. We have the same tools in our toolbox and we can use them, should use them, for every encounter. Does that get you as excited as it does me?

How are you using your words today? Do they lift you and others up?

When I was a child, I grew up in what I now call a "hostile word environment." The models I had around me were pretty darn negative. I remember how my own friends, at times, didn't want to be around me because of my negative attitude. Believe it or not, I grew up with "the sky is falling Henny Penny" approach to everyday living. This influence rubbed off in every part of my life.

I didn't need enemies; I was hard enough on myself. Speaking something positive usually started with "I'm so dumb" or "I'll never be able to....because I can't...." My life was more about what I couldn't do than what I could, which was usually self-imposed. I remember how lonely I felt. Hope was something I didn't understand for many years.

Thankfully, as a youth I found myself going to church with the neighbors or friends from school. I looked for opportunities to be in church as a young person, even when my family mocked my efforts. What I remember in those early years was the amazing light that people in church had on their faces. People talked to me about hope and love like I had never heard before. By the grace of God, I learned that there was a different way of being in the world, and that I could have what they had.

It took many years to truly get rid of the old mind tapes of negativity and replace them with new DVD's of positive, affirming words, thoughts and images. I went from feeling totally victimized by my childhood, to walking out the victories of Christ in my life. There was a process I went through for letting go of negative thoughts (that consumed my days) and removing destructive words from my vocabulary.

> I went from feeling totally victimized by my childhood, to walking out the victories of Christ in my life.

During the change process, I held onto the "I was created for more" truth. God didn't design me to feel less than anything or anyone. He did not put me on earth to wait for the sky to fall. He put me here to be a light for other people to see His mercy and grace.

My victory is reminiscent of the movie "Titanic's" bow of the boat scene: arms stretched out, I declare, "I am Queen of my world!" As queen of my world, I get to use the power of my Almighty King to muster the words that set me free - for every situation!

So how do you begin your own self-talk and negative mindset transformation? The very first thing you must do is know that, beyond a shadow of a doubt, you were created for more. Know that you were designed with purpose and that you were bought by the blood of Jesus. When you truly get a hold of that truth, beyond all other knowledge, you can then begin your transformation process.

Here is a list of simple action steps that you might take to begin your own transformation process:

1. *Start paying attention to the people around you. Do they encourage you and others? Do they speak positively and from a place of love? We often act and react most like those we spend the most time with.*

2. *Ask those closest to you, even your boss or co-workers, how they perceive you. Do they see you as an encourager of others or as a Negative-Nellie? Reflect back on what people have said about you in the past as well. Often we have signs waving at us that we overlook.*

3. *Begin a journal of conversations to yourself about what you want in your lifetime. Spend a few minutes each day writing down the thoughts you have at that moment or from the day. Don't over analyze them, just write them down. After a few weeks, go back and read what you've been writing. Are you affirming where you want to go in life? Are you speaking hope and possibility? To change our mindsets and words means getting to a place where we can catch ourselves acting in the manner we most want to change, then we know how to adjust our path.*

4. *Get in the Word and begin to read everything you can about the power that is given to you by the blood of Jesus. Read how God uses the spoken word to create, give life and death. Pray to God to reveal where in your life you may be missing the mark with your self-talk and negative mindsets. God may have been sending signs to you for some time now; stop and listen, pay close attention to hear from Him.*

5. *Post notes of affirmation and positive words around your home, office, bathroom and even your car. The best way to transform where you are, to where you want to be, is through affirmations and action steps. So write down, and make plain, the desires of your heart for this internal change and speak it over yourself every day. His Word is for you too, so speak love, life and peace over yourself daily. Affirm the direction you want to go and you will soon follow it.*

When you begin your journey to transform your self-talk, you may find resistance from those closest to you. That resistance comes from their fear of your change. Remember that you were created for more, so don't allow the nay-sayers to pull you back. Stand up! Either they will come along side to support you, or you may need leave them behind. Keep your focus on what God has put in your heart and you will be victorious!

Kicking Fear Out

Fear is real.
It can stop you.
It can cause you to doubt.
It can debilitate you, emotionally, spiritually and even physically.
However, only if you allow it to.

You have the power to neutralize fear through knowing who you are in Christ. Whether it's real or imagined, fear is an enemy to your destiny and you must overcome its hold. It's one of the enemy's main weapons against us!

Know your enemy and how you are sensitive to its devices, and then fight back. Use Ephesians 6 as your guide for battle. Philippians 4 and Psalm 91 will also help calm your mind. You do not need to live with fear paralyzing you anymore. As a co-heir with Jesus Christ, the power and name of Jesus is your strength.

I've never thought of myself as a fearful person, until recently when I had a very interesting experience. There was a period of time when my back hurt for eight months straight. I couldn't figure out why it was hurting. I didn't have a new office chair, new mattress or anything else. Whether I exercised or not, sat in my massage chair or went to the chiropractor, it hurt continuously.

I also had an underlying level of anxiety that would never fully go away. I attributed that perpetual nervousness in the pit of my stomach to pushing myself out of my comfort zone on a regular basis. Little did I know that fears had been building up; fears about my kids, about safety, about doubts, about what if's, about many other little things. *Fear was gripping me, literally.*

One Saturday night church service, during a time of expressive worship, the pain fell off of me. At first, when I noticed my back didn't hurt any more

> Fear was gripping me, literally.

117

after service, I wasn't sure what had happened. I wasn't sure I believed it yet, and didn't say anything to my husband until two hours later.

During the next several weeks, God showed me it was fear being broken off during that time of worship. I understand now how sensitive I am to it, and that I need to guard my heart diligently so it does not attach to me again. In Jesus' name, I have authority over fear and I choose to say "NO" to it.

Like faith, fear is a force that can cause things to happen; negative things. Feelings of fear can create health problems, emotional stress, interrupted rest, reduced job performance, relationship strain, controlling behavior, inaction, and more. Those are real things.

In contrast, faith can also cause real things to happen like physical healing, a mind at ease, good decisions to be made, a good night's sleep, perseverance, a positive attitude, solutions to problems, praying, creativity, and more. In my experience, God's truth is the only thing that drives out fear.

To move forward and share your gifts without fear, you can remind yourself of, and renew your mind with, these thoughts:

- When I operate in my gifting, God can work through me, increasing my effectiveness.
- I can do all things through Christ who strengthens me.
- If I please God, my presentation, interaction, project, ministry, etc., is a success.
- I may not feel completely self-confident about my skills, but I can be confident that God is for me, and knows what He is doing.
- I will fear no evil, for You, God, are with me.
- Sharing my gifts with others not only gives my own soul satisfaction, but it also makes a positive impact on those around me.
- I will not be directed by fear, but by faith.
- This is what I was made for. This fits me perfectly.
- I won't depend on validation from people. The Lord will validate.
- Who I am is not all about me.
- I am the righteousness of God, in Christ Jesus.
- When I worry, I waste my thoughts.

This last thought, "when I worry, I waste my thoughts," is an interesting one. Let me share a quick story about the lesson I learned on that.

When my son was three, he had a few nights of bad dreams about skunks. Yes, the stinky black and white forest animals, which he had never actually seen in real life before. He may have watched an animal show and heard about them there, but in any case, skunks were plaguing his dreams.

In the dreams, skunks were coming into his room. He and I talked about how there was no way that could happen. My logical explanations didn't seem to help much, and he kept going on about his fears. Finally, I said this to him, "Honey, skunks are never going to come into your room. It's just not going to ever happen. When you worry about this all the time, you are wasting your thoughts."

As soon as those words escaped my mouth, "you are wasting your thoughts," God's Spirit taught me a lesson. How many times do I worry about things and waste my thoughts? What do I waste my thoughts about? What is my brain-power being used for? Am I meditating on fears and worries that don't really have any chance of happening? Even if there is a chance of them happening, is this what I want to focus on? Do I trust God in faith, or cling to my fearful thoughts?

I can't tell you the number of times God has taught me lessons like that through my children. Whether it's bad dreams or nervous reality, we are wise to move past the fears and obstacles, into purpose. Otherwise, worry saps our mental and physical energy, and the bad dreams win.

In the next chapter, we'll talk more about things to watch out for during your journey to calling; many of which are rooted in fear and may attempt to stop your progress.

Summary

Each day, we encounter messages which contradict God's truth about us. To live His calling for you, you'll need to combat these wrong messages and renew your mind about who you really are. Change starts in our minds, moves to our hearts and then becomes an outward expression.

The specific ways in which your mind needs renewal is in the areas of:

- Trust
- Self-Image
- Hope and Faith
- Spoken Words
- Kicking Fear Out

Trust - Trust that when God calls you to step out, that He knows what He's doing.

Self-Image - God wants to change your self-image to match His image of who you are.

Hope and Faith - Having hope and faith is about believing a promise or having a vision from God for your future, then waiting for it to come to pass.

Spoken Words - Your words, the actual words that come out of your mouth, are a creative force that can make things happen (positive or negative).

Kicking Fear Out - Fear will try to derail your calling from within, if you let it.

God wants to use you for a special purpose, but first He must speak words of life to your spirit to empower you with hope, courage, strength and faith. With your help, He can renew your mind.

Prayer: *Living Water, pour over me and remove any impurities. Show me where fear or limiting beliefs are stopping me from stepping out and taking my place in Your plan Lord. I know You see all my potential and believe in me. Please help me to believe in myself, knowing that You are for me. I CAN do all things when You strengthen me and speak to me Lord. Speak to me now about how I see myself and how You see me.*

Ask yourself:

- How, when and in what way does fear try to cling to me?
- Will I agree with God's plan, even if it doesn't 'look' like what I was expecting?
- What words and phrases do I need to stop using? Which do I need to start using?

Affirmations:

I make decisions based on faith, not fear.

Hope and faith are my default way of thinking, and I trust God's plan for me.

I can do all things through Christ who strengthens me!

Next, I want to make you aware of other potential "dream killer" issues so that you can be on your guard, ready to move past them into your calling.

13.

Freedom from Dream Killers

"The thief comes only to steal and kill and destroy; I have come that they may have life, and have it to the full." – John 10:10 (NIV)

As we've already discussed, there are things in life that can impede our progress in the gift sharing arena. Let's quickly expose and review some things to watch out for. This first particular list deals with the thoughts we wrestle with in our own minds. It will take determination to overcome these challenges, so please be courageous and don't let them stop you. Once again, you will need to change your mind by renewing your mindset.

Internal Dream Killers

Dream killers that exist within, that most of us will (or have already) encounter at some point include:

1. **Fear.** The root of many of the self-imposed blocks and issues. Fears of various kinds will paralyze you if you allow them to. Take an honest assessment of your thoughts. Are they often fear-based? Battle them with God's truth, and in Jesus' name.

2. **Self-focus.** The only thing you can take credit for is being obedient, making a decision and taking action. Otherwise, never forget that your gift isn't meant for your own benefit alone, or forget Who your gift came from. You offer something to the world for their benefit.

3. **Self-doubts.** We all have them in various areas of our lives. If you've identified and developed your gift, do not doubt what God has given you. Do not expect perfection, even from yourself.

4. **Imperfection.** Not one of us is perfect, and it can be stressful to try and be! God does not expect perfection from you, so please do not use that as an excuse to remain idle. Also, circumstances and the timing of opportunities for stepping out may not seem perfect either.

5. **Unworthiness.** Feel privileged that God has chosen you to further His purposes on the earth. Are you worthy of that? Are any of us? Not really, but that's the point. He wants to use us anyway to show His might! If you struggle with feelings of unworthiness because of past sin, failure or shame, have an answer from God's Word when the negative thoughts come in. Speak back to the accusations with verses like: I am a new creation in Christ, I am more than a conqueror through Him who loves me, for I know the plans He has for me for prosperity, hope and a good future, I have received forgiveness of my sins and a place among those who are sanctified by faith in Jesus.

You have received forgiveness and have a place!

6. **Insignificance.** To God, *you* are very significant. Maybe you've felt insignificant in the past, but that is not the truth. You are a very important person with special work to do. Even if you've experienced insignificance through negative relationships with people, God has a significant, good work planned for you. Will you choose to believe that truth?

7. **Wrong motives.** Whether it's fame, money, position or power, wrong motives can sneak in at any moment if we're not careful. Remind yourself that "it's not about me." *We must decrease, so He can increase.* God sees our hearts. God can cleanse your motives if you remain humble and understand where your help comes from. Apart from Him, we can do nothing, so keep your heart upon His altar. Choose to work His plan for the Kingdom's gain, instead of working your own plan for your own gain. God knows what you need and will supply it.

> We must decrease, so He can increase.

8. **Timidity.** I completely relate to this one. Timid people freeze up and have difficulty expressing themselves. Timid people do not step out and take their places. Practice expressing yourself in healthy ways. Open your mouth, take a step out, grow, share your heart - you've got something to say. God will help you to find your voice!

9. **Vain ambition.** This one is worldly. Yes, deep inside we all want to have good success. Let's not focus on worldly goals, self-seeking fame and attitudes. Instead, we aim for true significance, humility and remaining open to what God has for us. This one is connected to wrong motives and stems from selfishness. Selfishness never results in living a life of significance.

"I pursued a paycheck for so long in my life, rather than pursuing the ultimate assignment from God in my life." – Derrick Miles

10. **Procrastination.** This one seems innocent enough, but may have some roots in fear for some people. Either that, or just bad habits! For those of us who are serious and passionate about discovering, developing and sharing our gifts, procrastination should have no place in our lives. It's a seemingly nice, less blatantly sinful, way of never stepping out.

11. **Laziness.** Laziness is like a cancer that eats away at prosperity in all areas of life; family, career, business, finances, health, etc. If you struggle with laziness, only you have the power to change, and to remove this serious success-blocking mindset or lifestyle.

12. **Past failures.** We have all experienced failure in life and have fallen short. Who knows how many times I've failed at things in the past, but there have been many. God gives you grace when you fail, and wants you to get up, make the necessary adjustments, and keep walking the path He's placed before you.

    Memories of past failures hold our future hostage. At times, failures plague our memories, stopping us from trying anything "risky" again.

    - "I failed before, what makes me think I won't fail again?"
    - "Can I really discover my gifts? Even if I do, how do I know I can share them effectively in the world?"
    - "My track record is not good so far. I feel like a failure."
    - "I'm not sure God can use, or rely on, someone like me."

    Fear of failure is actually a self-preservation mechanism that our minds have. Your mind says, "I risked something before and had a negative result. Note to self: Stay in the safe zone." Unfortunately, it can end up working against us.

Note to new self: "Failures are just an opportunity to do a course-correction and get better; *for though a righteous man falls seven times, he rises again* (Proverbs 24:16 - NIV). God is with me."

Don't be a person who gives up easily. Too many others throw in the towel at the first sign of difficulty, so those who persevere have the advantage. Even if we have to pick ourselves up after multiple failures, let us continue to run the race. Back in school, failing may have been unacceptable, but in life, it's inevitable. Fail forward and keep going!

13. **Fear of Success.** Some people fear success. Why?

   - Some have fears about what their close relationships might think if they had success. "If I succeed, I may make others around me feel bad."
   - Others self-sabotage good situations and progress because of limiting beliefs they have about themselves.
   - Feelings of unworthiness or fears about recognition may trip some people up.
   - Being successful often includes the idea of becoming wealthy and having a lot of money. Having money makes some people apprehensive.
   - Some people are afraid of success because they think it will pull them away from God.
   - Additionally, success brings added responsibility with it, which some would rather not manage.

   Whatever your definition of success is, it should include using your God-given gifts and operating in His calling for you. God wants you to use your gifts well, and that should result in you seeing good success in various ways. That is a good thing! You are made to make a difference.

14. **Irrational Emotions.** People who allow their feelings to take them on emotional roller coaster rides usually remain fairly ineffective in life. Emotions serve an important purpose for us, but the key word is "serve." If your emotions rule you, you will lack stability and

reliability. It may also cause you to feel like a victim in life rather than having logical control of your choices and decisions.

One way to stop being tossed back and forth by winds of emotion is to filter them through the truth of God's Word. When a strong emotion comes up, pay attention to it. Figure out where the root of it is coming from. Is it valid? Is it helpful? Is it hurtful? Is it based on truth? Have a strong foundation of truth and purpose in your heart so that the emotional storms of life will not sway you when bad days come.

15. **I Can't.** My kids make that statement, and it is like fingernails on a chalkboard! Many of us adults still embrace it too. As we grow up, we take on the bad habit of telling ourselves we "can't." Take an honest look at your life and what you tell yourself you can't do. Is it really that you "can't," or more truthfully that you won't or just don't want to?

"I can't do that." Really?

Now, it is a true statement if I say I can't physically lift a car. However, it is not a true statement if I say, "No, I can't come speak to your group" or "I can't join that team." True statements would be, "I could come speak, but I won't because it is not my core demographic," "I don't want to spend my time that way" or "I don't feel ready for that yet." You have the power of choice!

Many times, using the "I can't" phrase swindles your power and leaves you feeling like a victim. By using it, you limit yourself and put a cap on your potential, as well as feeling like your power of choice has been stolen.

In most cases, embracing the desire to live your everyday calling means giving up saying "I can't." There's a freedom that comes when you get clarity about God's gifts and purpose for you. It helps you honestly respond to others who make requests of you that don't fit. It gives you a clear path to operate on. It also changes your perspective about what you're capable of.

> *"…serve him with wholehearted devotion and with a willing mind, for the LORD searches every heart and understands every desire and every thought."* – 1 Chronicles 28:9 (NIV)

External Dream Killers

Aside from the self-imposed or inner blocks that get in the way of stepping out, there may be outside forces that we'll contend with as well. What are they? Here are a few examples:

1. **People Who Influence Our Lives.** Do the people around you support your destiny? Are the people close to you telling you, "you can do it" when you step out boldly to share your gifts? If not, they may be the crabs pulling you back into the pot. The thought of your success and growth either frightens them (because they think you will outgrow them), or challenges them because they themselves are idle (and they don't want to change).

   Those who you allow to influence your life (attitudes, activities, values, self-esteem, etc.) should be building you up, not tearing you down. Reject the influence of those who hold you back from being all that God created you to be. *Accept the influence of those who have your best interest in mind, and influence you from a place of love.*

   > Accept the influence of those who have your best interest in mind, and influence you from a place of love.

2. **Spiritual Warfare.** Although I can't claim to be an expert in this area, I know spiritual battles and attacks happen, even to people of God. The enemy will try to come against people who are taking ground for good. I must say though, in many cases the enemy gets too much credit.

   > *"Here is one thought to consider when trying to evaluate if you are, in fact, experiencing spiritual warfare: "Before we launch out in aggressive warfare, we must realize that many of our battles are merely the consequences of our own actions."* – Pastor Francis Frangipane

   Natural consequences for bad decisions cause many of our woes. Having said that though, true spiritual warfare *is* serious business.

Your mind and thought life can be potential targets, as well as relationships and circumstances. We have an enemy who does not want us to help advance the work of the Lord.

What can you do? Pray, study the Bible, speak words of faith and God's promises, fast, anoint people or things with oil, take disturbing thoughts captive, take communion, and seek counsel from spiritually wise people who can help you. God has given you power and authority because of who you are in Him, so learn how to use your authority well. There is power in the name of Jesus!

3. **Negativity.** Being around negativity can really be a brain-drain and a dream-stealer. When possible, separate yourself from relationships that heap condemnation on you or fester with gloom. Negativity is catchy, and we can even find ourselves mimicking negative thoughts and attitudes and perpetuating them if we're not careful.

   Are you the one who is negative? If you are concerned that you might be the negative person in your relationships, ask someone who will tell you the truth. Negativity springs up from what you believe in your heart. Negative self-talk and self-esteem leads to spoken words and attitudes, which come out based on the negative expectations or a negative vision that you hold on to for your future.

   Another aspect of negativity is a "can't-do" attitude. You can tell when negativity is affecting you, because you may feel deflated, hopeless or devalued. Refuse to accept the negativity from others into yourself, and don't feed on it. Choose to hold on to hope and faith, no matter what is "seen."

4. **Health Problems.** Whether it's your own health or a loved one's, health problems or accidents strike at inopportune times. It may feel like a frustrating setback. If you are ailing, or find yourself consumed with caring for someone else who is, your purpose for that time period is regaining health and getting or giving care. It's a time for learning and strengthening, both physically and in faith. Ask yourself, how can you still use your gifts during this time period?

5. **Competing Priorities/Activities.** Do you have time termites? Pesky time termites are all the little things we waste our time with instead of making headway with our gifts and calling. They include things like television, online social networking, magazines, excessive grooming or cleaning, mindless entertainment, window shopping, email, video games, addictions, texting, etc. They're definitely creatures of habit!

But seriously, we all need to take an honest look at how we spend our time and prioritize our activities. If an unnecessary activity competes for the time we should spend using or developing our gifts, it should go. Give highest priority to activities that produce results and move you closer to your goals.

Being too busy, even with worthwhile activities, eats up precious time when we should be focusing on other, more specific actions. Remember your priorities and what you place high value on in your life. I've been guilty of this on many occasions, but lately *I've decided to say "no" to good ideas, so I can remain focused only on the God ideas.*

"Most of us are busy, but undisciplined. We are active, but not focused. We are moving, but not always in the right direction. By creating a stop-doing list as well as a to-do list, you will bring more discipline and focus into your life." – Jack Canfield

> I've decided to say "no" to good ideas, so I can remain focused only on the God ideas.

6. **Pressure to Conform or Expectations of Others.** Other people have an image of you and expectations of you; expectations about the way you look, behave, talk, work, and serve. Here is what you need to consider for yourself:

   - Am I conforming to the expectations of others, rather than to God's will?
   - Does the image that others have of me match who God sees me as?
   - Will I bow to the pressures and requests that others put on me, when they don't align with what God has for me?
   - Am I strong enough to throw off unhealthy expectations that others try to put on me?

- Can I say "no" to things I should not be doing?

Some of us fall into the trap of conforming to a role we're supposed to play because it either "looks" good, or someone else expects us to. Here's my thought on that: If it doesn't fit, don't wear it.

Remember the story of those red shoes that I bought on clearance? Wow, they were a great deal – only $7! The only problem is that they're a half size too small. Every time I put them on, I realize they don't fit me real well. In fact, they hurt. I'm forcing myself into wearing something that does not fit, and it's very uncomfortable.

Just like those shoes that aren't quite right for me, people often take on positions, tasks, projects, images, join committees, or accept other kinds of roles that do not really fit them. These wrong fit roles become time termites. Why do we do that?

- Maybe it is because the perfect fit hasn't come along yet so we impatiently settle for less?
- Maybe the role has a certain prestige or status associated with it so we take it, even though it steals time from our true calling and gifts?
- Maybe others expect us to take on a task, even when we know inside that it goes against God's will for us?
- Or maybe we are not aware of our gifts or purpose yet, so we flounder around, "trying on" anything that comes along. Been there…done that…

I don't mean to minimize the impact these internal and external challenges have on people. My point for writing short descriptions and suggestions is this: I could go on and on about fears and things that stop us. Let's not dwell there. You already know which things on that list attempt to hinder you. I already know what tries to stop me. Preferably, let's focus on becoming aware, growing and renewing our minds where needed instead, then move forward with discovering, developing and sharing our gifts. The world is waiting for your awesomeness!

Summary

Be aware of, and on-guard against, issues, traps and challenges (either internally or externally) that will attempt to stop your spiritual journey.

Potential internal dream killers include things like:

1.	Fear	9.	Vain ambition
2.	Self-focus	10.	Procrastination
3.	Self-doubts	11.	Laziness
4.	Imperfection	12.	Past failures
5.	Unworthiness	13.	Fear of success
6.	Insignificance	14.	Irrational emotions
7.	Wrong motives	15.	"I Can't"
8.	Timidity		

External dream killers may be things like:

1. People who influence our lives
2. Spiritual warfare
3. Negativity
4. Health problems
5. Competing priorities/activities
6. Pressure to conform or expectations of others

Prayer: *Loving God, thank You for hiding me in the cleft of Your Rock. You are good, all the time. Let Your truth live within me, and remove any strongholds in me that the enemy may try to manipulate. Tear down anything in my life that would try to exalt itself against You and Your Word. Help my heart meditate on Your truth at all times.*

Ask yourself:

- What internal dream killers try to stop me from my calling?
- Can I identify the external dream killers that hinder my progress?
- Do I hold on to any of these dream killers purposefully? If so, why?

Affirmations:

Fear does not stop me from moving forward.
The opinions of others do not control me, but God's will moves me.
God has a prosperous future for me, full of hope and good things.

14.
Up-Level Development

*"Move out of your comfort zone. You can only grow
if you are willing to feel awkward and uncomfortable
when you try something new."* – Brian Tracy

Get ready to up-level your game if you desire to *Step Out and Take Your Place*. As I mentioned previously, stepping out requires growth, which will cost you time, effort and probably money. You can count on it costing you one more thing too: Your comfort zone. Expect to move out of your comfort zone, and the one after that, and the one after that!

Comfort Zone Expansion

"They go from strength to strength..." – Psalm 84:7a (NIV)

As I look back on my life, I can identify comfort zones that I've camped in, meaning time periods when I was stagnant and not growing, not seeking the Lord or challenging myself. There have been a lot of them though, that have come and gone. Although it's cozy and familiar, my current one is fading away...Can you relate?

My friend and pastor's wife, First Lady Tomekia Williams, has been on a long journey with God. Through His call, and her answering that call, Tomekia's life has been transformed.

It has been seventeen years now that I have been walking with the Lord. During the first one-third of that time, I had no idea the future would include God calling me to preach. I was very much like Moses, with all his various life issues and self-doubts.

His innate gifts had already been placed in me, as they are in all of us. Even though the gifts and calling I had were there already, they were not ripened. I had to get to know Him more, and my development stages were much like a baby getting ready to walk.

God used and worked out the circumstances in my life to help with developing my calling. He spoke to me in dreams. I felt driven to study the Word. I even felt prompted to speak messages and speak out loud to my walls. I attended the school of life through the Holy Spirit.

Now as pastors, my husband and I try to create a church environment for growing gifts. We encourage people to test out their gifts within the church, and do some trial and error. Like King David, we all go through a series of events to reach our "wealthy place" – the place of fullness and little lack.

Obviously, comfort zones are comfortable. Thus, moving out of them will feel...uncomfortable. Growing takes great faith and persistence.

Comfortable involves: Routine, expected outcomes, static skill level, receiving, easy, contented, undemanding, habits, old thoughts, and sharing your gifts at a comfortable level.

Uncomfortable involves: Change, new knowledge and understanding, change in commitments or priorities, unknown, risk, giving, new disciplines, renewing the mind, and sharing your gifts at a challenging or new level.

I'm not sure if Tomekia has any comfort zone left at this point, since she's pressed through so many thus far! However, let me add that she (and you) always has a comfort zone within the arms of the Lord. Even if our circumstances continue to evolve and fluctuate, we're always safe and secure in our relationship with Him.

*"You will increase my honor and comfort me
once more."* – Psalm 71:21 (NIV)

God will not leave you or forsake you as you step out. On the contrary! I imagine it's like teaching a child to ride a bike, and as we move to the next level of our potential and capacity in our calling, the bikes get bigger and more complex.

We nervously start with the training wheels and helmet, clumsily rocking side to side as we pedal slowly forward. God runs alongside, cheering us on with words of encouragement. As soon as we're ready, and He knows exactly when that is, He moves us to the next phase - no training wheels!

Our safety net training wheels are gone (oh no!), and we're not sure we want to move at all. God grabs onto the back of the seat and starts the momentum, as we omit a panicky shriek. We have simultaneous emotions of fear, excitement, self-doubt, and hope. As we ride on under His careful watch, a sense of accomplishment comes.

We get better, improve and begin feeling comfortable with our new aptitude. We test out all the tricks and paths, test the limits and learn a few lessons. When we fall, God is right there to see how we react and to pick us up and brush us off when needed.

Then one day we realize we've outgrown the first bike. It cramps our growing legs which are capable of more, and it's time for the next level. Once again, making a change makes us nervously excited. God knows all the ins-and-outs of the next-size-up bike, with its gears, features and performance parameters. Sometimes we already assume we know it all, and skip His valuable advice, only to meekly return later to solve a problem we've gotten ourselves in to.

This cycle continues through many levels, until we are lean, strong and honed, riding on a high-performance racing bike. God coaches us, mind, body and spirit, to ride the race in the right direction and to our full potential.

Assume you are the child on the bike. What was your role here? *To listen, get on, ride, trust God, and keep riding.* Yes, God has grace for our mistakes and inadequacies, but He wants to see us persevere and not quit. If we fall, He wants to help us up and see us keep going. If we make a wrong turn, He calls out to redirect us onto the right path. If we hit the ditch, we should not remain there.

One of my speaking and business coaches, Teri Hawkins, challenged me and a small group of speaking professionals with this message one day:

Did Iacocca ever quit? Did Claiborne ever give up? Did Jordan ever throw in the towel? In our society we would like to say, "Of course not!" We want them to be superlative; to be someone special. We want to sit in our loungers and cheer them on, read about their latest win and admire their most recent creation. This, of course, allows us to justify why we are not walking fully in our own greatness. We talk amongst ourselves and agree that although we are happy for them, and know they worked hard, some people are just given more than others. Maybe they had money on their side, knew the right people, had the education, or were born with the talent.

Let me answer the question I asked you above. The answer is "yes." I know for a fact that Lee Iacocca has quit, that Liz Claiborne gave up in her life and that Michael Jordan has thrown the towel in when things got tough. The difference for these three leaders of their world is that they found quitting poisonous to their dreams, to their desires, to who they wanted to be. They learned how to make commitments in order to prevent quitting from ruining their dreams.

There are many forms of quitting. Within each form, you will find masterful justifications employed to convince all comers that the quitting was justified. I want to tell you it is not! Do not justify your quitting. Admit you quit. When you do this, you will not like yourself so much. You will feel uncomfortable, maybe disgusted, angry or sad. These are the very things that give you the motivation to learn how to commit so that you never quit again.

And now I must say something that might hit a sore spot for you: Stop quitting on yourself. If you are afraid to make a phone call, and so have not – you have quit. If you like the idea of how to get clients, but you do other things before making contact – you have quit. If you keep putting off stepping forward until all is perfect – you're quitting on yourself. The minute you decide to walk through the fire of your fears, you will begin to soar.

> Stop quitting on yourself.

Decide to change. I want you to learn how to commit and not quit.

Sometimes, the truth hurts, but I always appreciate it when it comes from a wise person with my best interests in mind. This message was a "time to get out of your comfort zone" message for me. Even reading it was uncomfortable. However, it was meant to stir up the comfortable people, moving them to the next level. It worked!

> *"And we urge you, brothers and sisters, warn those who are idle and disruptive, encourage the disheartened, help the weak…"* – 1 Thessalonians 5:14a (NIV)

I've decided that what God wants is what I want. I made that decision when I began my own journey to seek God about His calling on my life. Even so, at every stage the temptation to stop or quit has been there.

"Oh, I'm busy right now with x, y and z, so I'll get to this someday."
"I'm not sure I want to commit to growth because it requires too much effort."
"Maybe I can put off this intimidating task for a while."
"The latest and greatest idea has drawn me away and distracted me."
"Let me just settle down in my comfort zone and do the bare minimum that I can get away with."

Seriously, I've had all these thoughts at one point or another during my journey. Maybe you have too. Nevertheless, all of these responses leave a person's soul frustrated, knowing something is missing.

Inspired or Dedicated?

Inspiration plays an important role in our lives. *When we're inspired by something or someone, this inspiration shows us the areas where we may desire change, brings an awareness of what awakens our spirit and allows us to dream.*

However, there's a big difference between inspiration and dedication. Anyone can be inspired temporarily through an emotional or motivational message. On the other hand, dedication is a developed character trait based in perseverance and passion. Think about these two in terms of seeds. Inspiration sits on the surface; dedication has roots. Inspiration has the potential to take root, but only if it's drawn into the soil, taken in and nurtured.

> When we're inspired by something or someone, this inspiration shows us the areas where we may desire change, brings an awareness of what awakens our spirit and allows us to dream.

When a person becomes inspired to accomplish, learn or do something, one of these two things will happen:

1. The inspiration and motivation fades. The birds (fears) come and snatch up the seeds of inspiration, or the seeds rot on the surface where they fell (idleness or boredom).

2. Inspiration turns into dedication. Dedication causes a "no-quit" resolve. The seed falls on good ground, that's ready to receive it, and take root.

Have you been inspired to move forward with something, but then didn't? I have, numerous times; to exercise more, to keep up with business expenses on a weekly basis, to pre-plan healthy meals for my family, to join a volunteer team, etc. I'm sure you have as well. However, I am dedicated to using my gifts and living my everyday calling. For me, that's become non-negotiable. There's a big, fat root of dedication in that area that will not be neglected.

Through this book, I desire to go beyond simply inspiring you. I want to see you become dedicated to your calling-discovery journey.

This is my advice: Nurture dedication when it comes to your calling. It takes dedication to discover your gifts, to develop them and especially to share them with the world. A big difference between those who are successful in this life and those who aren't depends on dedication, which includes devotion, commitment and enthusiasm.

When you're passionate about something, that passion keeps you going. Your gift will burn inside you to be used, especially when you're aware of it. You can't help it. It calls to you. When you don't use it, you feel hollow and dry inside.

What will you choose? To be inspired by this book and ultimately do nothing, or to be dedicated to going on the journey with God? The power of choice that we each have is life-altering!

You cannot get to operate in God's calling for you by staying comfortable. Not quitting takes a commitment, and also trust in God that He has your best interests in mind for your future. He calls, and you ride on.

Stay committed to:

- Seeking God
- Spiritual Growth
- Personal Growth
- Renewing Your Mind
- Developing Your Gifts
- Stepping Out to Take Your Place

You are more than you know, and it's your job to find out what it is that you don't know yet. Keep expanding the borders of your comfort zones. Press on; keep going and growing!

Summary

Stepping into your calling requires growth, which will cost you time, effort and probably money. You can count on it costing you one more thing too: Your comfort zone. The Lord guides us from strength to strength, from glory to glory, growing and preparing us for His work. We always find comfort in Him, as He encourages us to ride at new levels.

Stay dedicated to growth and to your discovery journey with God. Don't quit! Make the decision that what God wants, is what you want too. Push any excuses you may have aside that tell you to stop your progression.

Inspiration is fleeting if it doesn't quickly transform into dedication. Inspiration opens a door to dream, and dedication is what will make you walk through that door.

Prayer: *Help me Father. Give me a spirit of endurance and dedication to Your purposes. Stir me up on the inside and speak to my heart and mind. Give me the courage I need to move out of my comfort zone, and into Your calling for me. I know You will always comfort me while encouraging me to expand. I am dedicated to You, Father.*

Ask yourself:

- Am I willing to move out of my comfort zone, towards God's calling for my life?

- What am I not willing to do that's keeping me from stepping out into my calling?
- Do I give up easily when something gets hard, or if there's no immediate gratification? Why?

Affirmations:

God is where I find my comfort.
God has grace for me.
I relentlessly pursue God's purposes for me.
I do not quit!
What God wants is what I want.

15.

Embrace Your Inner Leader

Before starting my calling discovery journey with God, I never considered myself a leader, in any area of my life. Without a doubt, viewing myself in this new way is one of the biggest lessons I've learned and mind shifts I've made during this process.

If you're anything like me, getting a new "leader" self-image is a realization that changes your life forever. However, you may be thinking, "Does everyone have an inner leader? I'm not sure I do." I asked my friend, Dondi Scumaci, this question during a recent interview. Here is what she had to say:

We all have the opportunity to lead. Maybe we don't see ourselves as a leader with all things and with all people, but be aware of those moments when God is asking you to lead in specific situations.

Is He asking you to step up to the plate in certain situations and demonstrate leadership? Sometimes a leader is a catalyst for change by asking the right questions. Sometimes a leader delivers support at a critical moment and it empowers other people. Sometimes a leader speaks out against gossip or a wrong-doing. Sometimes the leader is the person who is washing the feet.

Leadership has a lot of faces to it, and we have the responsibility to explore those different avenues. Give yourself permission to develop your own leadership style.

I appreciate Dondi's perspective on this. She went on and dispelled some leadership myths many of us believe. For example, many of us think leaders must have all the answers, must motivate everyone around them, should look a certain way (e.g. wears a certain type of outfit or has a certain stature), or needs to have a loud, commanding presence. If we hold these beliefs and this specific image in our minds of what a leader must be, we may disqualify ourselves.

Believe me; you have a lot to offer. God knows you have a lot to offer. Even you probably know you have a lot to offer. You're free to lead with your gifts and calling in the way God directs you, rather than having to conform to an image of someone else's leadership style.

You Are Inspiring

Did you know that when you share your gifts, you inspire others? It's true. Think about how you feel when someone else shares their gifts.

- When a skilled, anointed worship leader shares her gift, the people who hear are inspired to open their hearts to God.
- When a creative financial thinker teaches others, it inspires others to move forward with financial planning when they've been stuck in that area.
- When a perceptive, caring counselor meets with a couple, marriages are saved from the brink of divorce.
- When a copywriter makes a business owner's website wording dance, the right message gets out to customers and a need in the marketplace is satisfied.
- When a local master of a traditional craft shares their work and passes down the knowledge, a cultural treasure endures and inspires others to learn about their heritage.
- When a naturopath or chiropractor uses their gift of physical healing, people formerly in pain have new hope and health.

Your calling will inspire others too. Pray that it also leads them to grow roots of dedication to the things of God. When other people around me use their gifts, it never ceases to amaze me. I'm so thankful and appreciative of the gifts they're sharing with me and excited because their willingness to share shows obedience to God. Leaders inspire others!

I want to share a story with you that shows how your calling and gifts inspire other people. This true story is from author, Jack Canfield. Through the *Chicken Soup for the Soul* book series that he co-authored, he's seen lives drastically changed.

What happens when people do find "it" and reach their calling? As an example of my work, I'd like to give you the story of a woman named Susanna Crowder. Susanna was homeless and pregnant, and she was literally on the street, living in doorways at night. She was dumpster diving behind McDonalds, and would go to the library during the day to get out of the cold.

She got so depressed that she decided that when the baby was born, she was going to kill herself. She worked out a plan with the other street people that she would deliver the baby, give it to one of them to take to the hospital, and then she would then crawl through a hole in a fence, crawl onto the railroad tracks and let a train run her over. This was all planned out. Within the next week or two, she was going to deliver.

One day, she went in to the library to get out of the cold, and they were setting up a display table up front full of inspirational books. She said, "I just grabbed one without looking at it, because I just wanted any book to read so they wouldn't throw me out."

She sat down and starting reading the book. It was my Chicken Soup for the Soul book. She opened it up to a story called "Puppies for Sale," which is about a dog born with hip dysplasia. A kid fell in love with this puppy, and she said to herself, "My God, if that puppy that was not formed correctly could be loved unconditionally by a human being, perhaps there is hope for me."

She decided not to commit suicide, and within a year, she bought a home and started her own soup kitchen for the homeless. Now she is working with Harvard professors and retired economic professors setting up new kitchens. They don't just feed people, but they also feed their souls with chicken soup stories. Once she found her purpose, her life literally took off from being a person on the street to one of the most passion-producing people on the planet because she found hope, and knew this hope needed to be shared with others.

Jack shared his messages of hope, inspiration and love through his book which impacted Susanna. Susanna turned around and discovered purpose in her life and now helps and inspires the lives of others. It would be interesting to hear a story from someone whose life has benefitted from her work, who has now discovered their own calling in life too.

Do you see the process of "paying it forward" happening? What if Mr. Canfield had decided not to write his book? Or, what if he had written it, but then gave up on it because it wasn't selling? He shared this with me, *"You know, we couldn't sell it for a year-and-a-half. No one wanted to buy it, but we never gave up. I just knew it was part of my destiny and we stuck with it."*

141

When you share your gifts, other people will thank you. *When you operate in your calling, it influences the lives of others in potentially life-changing ways.* In doing so, you'll be seen as a leader in the area of your gifting, and people may look to you for guidance and help.

> When you operate in your calling, it influences the lives of others in potentially life-changing ways.

Does it concern or scare you to be called a leader? Well, guess what - You already are! As a person of faith, it's interesting to discover that people are watching you. They've been paying attention and expect something peculiar from you, simply because you're known as a Christian. In fact, some of these observers may even be disappointed or indignant when we look (our behavior, words, actions, character, faithfulness, level of peace, etc.) no different than the world. I have a personal story about that very experience.

In 2005, when our church started implementing their small groups program, my husband, Chris, and I were asked if we could host a small group in our home. We agreed, and for a while had just one other couple who came regularly. They were not regular church attenders. We had known this couple for quite a few years, shared meals together, game nights, and Chris and I had actually worked with the husband at a previous job.

One evening, our small group topic was "mentoring." After we watched our DVD presentation by our Associate Pastor, we had discussion questions. One of the questions on the sheet was, "Who are your mentors?" Chris and I gave our answers, sighting various people like pastors, family members and past teachers. When it was the other couples' turn, the wife's answer completely caught me off guard. She said, "Well, I think you guys are."

My brain had to do a double-take, and I'm sure my face showed it! The husband chimed in and contemplatively said, "Yes, I think so. I know a lot of people who say they're Christians, but I think they're just Christians on Sunday mornings. You guys are the only ones we know who are really living your lives like Christians and walking the talk."

This very much surprised me, for two reasons. First, was the realization that other people had been paying attention and watching us. Secondly, I was disturbed by how many other people who are known as "Christians" are not taking their faith seriously. I always knew that was the case, but to hear someone outside of the church say it, brought it to the forefront.

People have an expectation of those who categorize themselves as Christians. They expect to see a noticeable different. Too many people carry the label only, but don't have an authentic relationship with Jesus that truly transforms them in a positive way. This is one of the sad reasons why people are turned off by Christianity, as they see it.

As a person of God, you're an automatic leader meant to inspire others. To be a leader is to set an example; not an example of perfection, but of vision, hope, dedication, and being authentic. You can still be the real you and be a leader. People appreciate leaders who are genuine and don't try to hide their flaws, because it gives them hope!

As you move through this journey of discovery with God, part of the eventual outcome will be to use your gifts with boldness, to everyday live out your calling, to guide and help others, then pass your wisdom on as a mentor. These actions definitely describe someone who leads. I pray that we can learn to lead in a way that's pleasing to the Lord.

> *"A man's gift makes room for him, and brings him before great men." –* Proverbs 18:16 (NASB)

Embrace your inner leader!

Take it from me, leadership attributes and characteristics *can* be learned, practiced and developed. Growing, learning and developing can feel scary and exciting at the same time. However, I'm living proof that a shy, quiet waif can bloom into a leader by following God's lead. First learn to follow God's Word and hear His voice, then learn to follow what He's placed in your heart. Remember, those who want to lead have first learned to follow.

This reminds me of a biblical leadership study I did for a class I took. Our assignment was to choose one leader from the Bible, study them and then do a 7-10 minute presentation about the person for the group. I chose Nehemiah as my leader to learn from.

I found so many nuggets of leadership wisdom that I didn't have time enough to use them all! As you may (or may not) already know, Nehemiah led and rallied thousands of Jews to rebuild Jerusalem's broken down walls. Here are several main concepts that I discovered:

- **Godly leaders are devoted to the things of God.**

As I read through Nehemiah, one main theme kept coming up. Nehemiah cared about the things God cares about. When he heard the news that Jerusalem's walls were "broken down, and its gates had been burned with fire," he wept and mourned. I can just imagine God's Spirit hovering over Jerusalem, the special city of His chosen people, and being grieved about it as well.

The wall around the city represented protection, dignity and strength. Without it, the city was vulnerable, embarrassing and weak. Nehemiah deeply cared about this city's welfare. God deeply cared about this city's welfare. Nehemiah felt passionate about seeing the city of his fathers restored to its full glory. God desired to see this city rebuilt, restored and re-inhabited by His people.

Remember when we discussed the Calling Components™ of interests and passions? This is a great example of having interests and passions that match God's. As we can see, Nehemiah and God cared about the same thing. Because of his devotion to the things of God, just like King David, Nehemiah could also be considered a man after God's own heart.

- **Leaders do not accept "less than."**

A leader makes people realize they don't have to accept less than God's best. Nehemiah challenged and inspired the people to take on a project that was for their own benefit!

He had never actually seen the city in this devastated state, but the mere thought of it brought him much grief, and then stirred him to action. Think about this: There was a remnant of Jews still living in and around Jerusalem who probably saw that broken-down, damaged city every day. Did they grieve about it when it first happened? Probably, but at some point it became normal. They got used to it. That's just the way it was, right?

If anything in our lives is broken-down, and is meant to be an inheritance from God, He always feels passionate about rebuilding it. God places the awareness of need on a person's heart, then waits for a builder to respond;

a builder who has a heart that cares about restoring broken-down inheritances.

This makes me ask myself, "What broken-down things have I gotten used to, that God wants to see rebuilt in my life?" Hmmm…interesting thought.

> If anything in our lives is broken-down, and is meant to be an inheritance from God, He always feels passionate about rebuilding it.

- **No previous leadership experience is necessary.**
That's right! As far as I can tell, Nehemiah had no previous leadership experience, whatsoever. There is hope for us! Nehemiah's position was the king's cupbearer, which means he was the one to bring drinks to the king. Basically, Nehemiah was the king's water boy! Yes, there was certainly prestige that went along with this position, and he did spend time in the king's presence regularly, but leadership? Nope. Honestly, this made me happy when I discovered it.

No matter what your background is, or is not, God will use you. All we need to have is a deep inner confidence that we've been called according to His purposes. When you have a Godly mandate (clear mission/calling), paired with upright character and dedication to the things of God, you can do all things through Him!

- **People follow leaders with a Godly mandate.**
Because of Nehemiah's clear, God-ordained vision, people partnered with him. Maybe your calling isn't to repair the broken down wall of a major city. Maybe your calling does not involve leading thousands of people in some massive project. However, I anticipate that your calling *will* involve partnering with, and influencing, others.

I don't know about you, but I can usually spot someone working on a God-idea right away. People with God-ordained missions stand out and attract attention. They draw people in because of their passion, devotion and purpose. I like to be working where God is working too.

Nehemiah gave them a clear call to action and appealed to their sense of what could (and should) be. He created, and included everyone in, a common vision. I respect that.

During this call to action, Nehemiah also made it clear that God was with him in this matter, not to mention that the king had also sent him. It took thousands of willing hands to complete this good work, none of which would have lifted a finger without one man's God-inspired calling.

- **Leaders stay focused.**

Nehemiah had a lot of people problems to deal with, many more people problems than he did project problems. In fact, his people problems included enemies outside of the Jewish community who made it their objective to purposefully intimidate, distract and discourage him. They did not want to see that wall rebuilt.

How many times do you and I get derailed because of challenges, opposition or distraction? I'm not sure I want to actually count my list of how many times that's happened, but here is what I learned: *Nehemiah did not allow discouragement, intimidation tactics or distraction to pull him away from his called work.* He maintained focus well.

The calling (vision, mission, purpose) that God gave Nehemiah was everything to him. Unfortunately, opposition and difficulty accompanied the whole process, but he persevered nonetheless. We would be wise to take this leadership principle into account. Stay focused, and don't allow anything to pull you away from the work you're called to, according to God's purposes! Opposition and challenges come with your calling!

> Nehemiah did not allow discouragement, intimidation tactics or distraction to pull him away from his called work.

"And we know that in all things God works for the good of those who love him, who have been called according to his purpose." – Romans 8:28 (NIV)

I hope this information inspires you like it did me. Leadership isn't about positions, titles, degrees, past leadership accomplishments, or fitting into a leadership style box. It's about running the good race, being dedicated to God and what He has called you to. You *are* a leader!

Summary:

Make the shift in your mind to view yourself as a leader. When expressed, the calling and gifts that you have will inspire others. People will look to you for guidance in the area of your gifts. Not only does your calling cause others to look to you, but the simple fact that you're a Christian means you are an automatic leader. People are observing you, looking to see a positive difference in your life.

Leadership skills and ability can be learned. Nehemiah was a great, biblical example of a leader with no previous leadership experience, who accomplished a massive project by staying dedicated to God and his calling. Like Nehemiah, you are called according to God's purposes, which will include influencing and helping others in some way. When you influence, you lead.

Prayer: *Father, You are working all things out for my good. Thank You! Lead me Lord. I pray that You complete the work You have started in me. Help me to see who I am in Your eyes. Help me to see myself as a leader, whether that be in big or small ways. Nonetheless, You command my destiny, and I trust in You. Use me for Your purposes.*

Ask yourself:

- Who might already see me as a leader?
- Can I identify with the label of "leader?" Why, or why not?
- In what way do I inspire others?
- Are there any broken-down inheritances that God has called me to rebuild?

Affirmations:

What God has called me to, He will equip me for.
I am a leader!
I influence others in a positive way that improves their lives.
I do not settle for "less than!"

Step Out – Operating in Your Everyday Calling

"By faith Abraham obeyed when he was called to go out to the place which he would receive as an inheritance. And he went out, not knowing where he was going." – Hebrews 11:8 (NKJV)

16.

How Your Calling Shows Up in the World

It's time for you to get ready to *Step Out and Take Your Place*! God has an inheritance for you in that place. Are you ready to step into it yet? Let's talk about what stepping out looks like.

Remember back in the Calling Components™ chapter, when we talked about different people having different combinations of components? Do you see how many combinations there could potentially be, and how they can shape a person's calling? We need your gifts, because they add a much-needed diversity within God's plan. At the same time, this gift diversity also creates a unity and collaboration within the body of Christ.

For example, imagine a band with twenty-five trumpets. It would be neat for about five minutes, but it would be much richer and beautiful to have three trumpets, three drums, three flutes, three clarinets, three trombones, three saxophones, three violins, three cellos, a piano, a tuba…you get the picture! In that case, a diverse set of instruments plays in unity to produce a purposeful melody. That is what the calling on our lives represent. God is our conductor!

God made you to express and operate in the world in a particular way, with a particular message to share, through using your gifts. What God has placed in you, and what He's called you to do with it, shows up in a unique way in the world.

How your calling shows up in the world will depend on these factors:

> God made you to express and operate in the world in a particular way, with a particular message to share, through using your gifts.

1. The Gifts or Calling Components™ that you have.

They are not by accident, and you will notice common themes as you start writing them out. Remember, your spiritual gifts are foundational.

2. The message that God has for you to share with others.

You have authority to speak this message because of either your past experiences, lessons learned, divine inspiration, and/or something you have overcome with God's help.

3. The way in which you are supposed to express yourself, and to whom.

You have a heart for a certain group, or groups, of people for some reason. You also have ways of expression that come naturally to you. Maybe it is through written or verbal forms, through movement, helping with your hands or by demonstrating.

Where do your gifts and calling apply?

> *"The person born with a talent they are meant to use will find their greatest happiness in using it."* – Johann Wolfgang Von Goethe

At the most basic level, your calling applies anywhere that God directs it to. When He's given you specific gifts, and you're willing to use them as He directs, He could prompt you to use them anytime, anywhere.

From another perspective, there's most likely a main environment, or a couple key environments, where God will position you to use your gifts.

It won't be limited to these key environments, but these may be the most obvious places God has placed you to use them in.

Potential physical locations to use your gifts and calling in:

- Home
- Church
- Work or Business
- Schools and Volunteering
- Neighborhood
- Online
- Mission Field
- Outdoors/Nature

Other possible environment examples:

- Within Relationships – with those you influence or lead, friendships, children, family, mentoring, one-on-one coaching, small groups, parenting, caregiving, etc.
- Communications (either virtual or in-person) – sharing wisdom, teaching, writing letters, writing books, blogging, speaking, conversations, counseling, encouraging or exhorting, singing, praying, etc.
- In Idea-Generating Situations – meetings, mastermind groups, focus groups, community forums, problem solving, crisis management, brainstorming sessions, tech "sandbox," etc.
- Creative Outlets – through art, music, dance, expressive visual performances, praise and worship, theatrical settings, on stage, poetry readings, contests, etc.
- Within Teams and Organizations – civic, sports, government, ministries, non-profits, music groups, etc.

When you show up in these environments, ready to use your gifts and to operate in your calling, what should you show up with?

- **Show Up With Confidence**

Some people seem to exude confidence. That hasn't been my experience in life! Sharing my gifts with confidence is where I had to do some serious inner work. Here are verses about confidence that still help me today:

> *"But blessed is the man who trusts in the LORD, whose*
> *confidence is in Him." –* Jeremiah 17:7 (NIV)

> *"So we say with confidence, "The Lord is my helper; I will not be*
> *afraid. What can man do to me?" –* Hebrews 13:6 (NIV)

Both of these verses include this thought: My confidence is in Him. Even when I didn't feel confident in my own abilities yet, I trusted God. Even in the areas where I do feel confident in my skills and abilities, it's still critical that I remain dependent on Him. What He has established and called me to do, He will help me with.

There is a boldness that's necessary to embrace before you can *Step Out and Take Your Place* with confidence. Even if you don't think of yourself as a bold person, trust me, there is a certain amount of boldness within each of us. Sometimes it comes out on its own when you least expect it. Sometimes you can dig deep within and pull it out when needed. After a while, it shows up more naturally.

Like I discussed in the Growth Section, my outer work, such as training, practice and skill building, prepared me to share my gifts. This development process did give me some confidence. However, I must say those sources of confidence were secondary to my confidence being rooted in God.

I know beyond a shadow of a doubt the work God has for me, and understand the gifts He's placed within me. That knowledge alone is the understanding that gives me the most confidence to step out and share.

• **Show Up With Humility**

As an instrument in His hand, remember where your help comes from. Remain humble, and always continue thanking God for the great things He has done. Yes, He used you to help and worked through you, but He always accomplishes His purposes, not us.

> *"Has not my hand made all these things, and so they came*
> *into being?" declares the LORD. "These are the ones I look*
> *on with favor: those who are humble and contrite in spirit,*
> *and who tremble at my word." –* Isaiah 66:2 (NIV)

Even though humility is a virtue that doesn't come naturally to most of us, at the heart of your calling discovery journey, the goal is not to exalt yourself. Instead, find yourself for His purposes. Through a thankful heart, God remains glorified.

Through your obedience to His call, His work is accomplished in homes, workplaces, businesses, relationships, churches, and lives. The temptation will be there to think more highly of yourself than you ought to, or to become closed-off to rebuke, correction or teaching from others. Fend off that temptation and show up clothed in humility. By being "clothed" in something, it means you purposefully had to put it on.

> *"Yea, all of you be subject one to another, and be clothed with humility: for God resisteth the proud, and giveth grace to the humble. Humble yourselves therefore under the mighty hand of God, that he may exalt you in due time"* – 1 Peter 5:5b-6 (KJV)

• **Show Up Knowing You've Been Provisioned**

God resources people whom He has called; those who have become qualified workers. I truly believe that a qualified worker receives the provision they need to complete their work.

What makes a worker qualified, you ask? In my prayer and journaling time a while back, God was showing me three main characteristics of a Kingdom worker who is qualified to be provisioned by Him. Here they are:

1. **Understand Purpose.** A qualified worker first needs to understand their calling and gifts, and how they fit with God's purposes. They know their life's mission and are ready to walk in it.

2. **Personal Character.** Secondly, a qualified worker has a strong moral character and is working towards becoming more Christ-like. They have personal integrity, faithfulness and capacity to care about what God cares about. Their heart is right!

3. **Trustworthy Stewardship.** The last, big characteristic has to do with a person's capacity to handle their blessings and what the Lord has entrusted them with. They've been found trustworthy in the small things, and therefore God sees they can be trusted with more.

A great example of being a good steward with the Lord's blessings is The Parable of the Talents found in Matthew 25 (NKJV):

"For the kingdom of heaven is like a man traveling to a far country, who called his own servants and delivered his goods to them. And to one he gave five talents, to another two, and to another one, to each according to his own ability; and immediately he went on a journey. Then he who had received the five talents went and traded with them, and made another five talents. And likewise he who had received two gained two more also. But he who had received one went and dug in the ground, and hid his lord's money.

After a long time the lord of those servants came and settled accounts with them.

So he who had received five talents came and brought five other talents, saying, 'Lord, you delivered to me five talents; look, I have gained five more talents besides them.' His lord said to him, 'Well done, good and faithful servant; you were faithful over a few things, I will make you ruler over many things. Enter into the joy of your lord.' He also who had received two talents came and said, 'Lord, you delivered to me two talents; look, I have gained two more talents besides them.' His lord said to him, 'Well done, good and faithful servant; you have been faithful over a few things, I will make you ruler over many things. Enter into the joy of your lord.'

Then he who had received the one talent came and said, 'Lord, I knew you to be a hard man, reaping where you have not sown, and gathering where you have not scattered seed. And I was afraid, and went and hid your talent in the ground. Look, there you have what is yours.'

But his lord answered and said to him, 'You wicked and lazy servant, you knew that I reap where I have not sown, and gather where I have not scattered seed. So you ought to have deposited my money with the bankers, and at my coming I would have received back my own with interest. So take the talent from him, and give it to him who has ten talents.'

'For to everyone who has, more will be given, and he will have abundance; but from him who does not have, even what he has will be taken away.'"

This traveling master entrusted his servants with something of value. In this case, it was money. God has entrusted each of us with valuable possessions of various kinds, including money, relationships, abilities and gifts too. He calls us to be good stewards of them. If we are not, we risk them being taken away. If we are, we make ourselves eligible to receive more.

When you understand your calling and God's purposes for your life, have strong Godly character and are a trustworthy steward of His blessings, you'll be provisioned with whatever is needed for the work He's called you to. Watch for His provision and resources. The resources, supply and opportunities may trickle in at first, but do not despise the small beginnings. Be faithful with a little and you'll become a qualified worker who gets more.

- **Show Up With Love**

In 1 Corinthians 12:4-6 (NIV), Paul writes, *"There are different kinds of gifts, but the same Spirit distributes them. There are different kinds of service, but the same Lord. There are different kinds of working, but in all of them and in everyone it is the same God at work."* Paul spends a great deal of time teaching the church about how vital an individual's role is within God's plan. Then, he adds how faith, hope and love play an important part in *how* we use our gifts.

In this section of the Bible, we see that Paul talks about having an attitude of love as we use our gifts, as we work and as we influence others around us. This reconciles who He has created us to be in the world, with the character God wants us to bring with as we go.

Loving someone and being loving (actions, behaviors, core being) are two very different things. I imagine that God hesitates to equip a loveless person with power. God *is* love. *To carry out our calling in life, as God desires, we need to show up with a spirit of love.*

- **Just Show Up**

> *"Most people go to their graves with their music still inside them."* – Oliver Wendell Holmes

> To carry out our calling in life, as God desires, we need to show up with a spirit of love.

To be able to *Step Out and Take Your Place*, you'll need to show up. I've heard people say that just showing up means victory for most of the battles you face in life! Sometimes showing up requires a sacrifice of time and effort; commodities that may seem depleted already.

That reminds me of a story that author Jack Canfield told me one day. Operating in his calling is hard, but rewarding work; work that he always shows up to.

My calling is that I am a teacher. I get excited when people wake up, when they feel empowered, when they take risks, when they're more authentic, when they realize they are valuable, when their self-esteem goes up because they realize they don't have to hold something against themselves for the rest of their lives. I want them to know they can live a full life and bring their gifts to the world. I believe everybody is born with a purpose and a set of talents that support that purpose. We can at least find out what that purpose is and what our talents are.

What brings you joy? What do you get excited about? Where do you find passion? I believe God put a guidance system within each one of us called joy. When you are doing what you are meant to do, you experience joy. It might be hard work, it might keep you up until 3:00 in the morning, but you love doing it.

When I am writing a book, sometimes I start writing at 9:00 at night, and the next thing I know, I hear birds singing and it's 6:00am. I haven't gone to bed yet! I am so engrossed in what I'm doing because it's so much fun. Even though it's work, even though it's hard, I still love the challenge of writing things in a way that people will actually get it.

For example, last week in Canada I was doing a seminar. I spoke right after a doctor who was speaking on health for one hour, then there was a twenty minute break, then I was to speak for two hours. In the middle of his talk, I was almost falling asleep. I had been working for two weeks straight without a day off on deadlines, writing, video recordings, working late, etc., and thought, "Am I going to make it? Here's this guy going before me and I'm already half-dead."

I walked on that stage and something happened. It's like someone plugs me in to a higher power. All the sudden I have this energy and it wakes me up. The doctor who preceded me, who I've known for years, said, "That was the most inspiring talk you've ever given. You were totally alive and I've never seen you so animated."

There's something I tap into when I'm doing what I'm supposed to do. I do what I do because I'm supposed to do it. When I do it, I am awake, I am alive, I'm happy, passionate, I know what to say and do, and I am guided at that moment. That's how I know I am on track.

I remember a woman came up to me at the end of a book signing event. We were there until about 11:45 at night. She said, "I could have listened to you all night." I said, "I could have spoken all night." That's the way I feel. I'm never ready to stop and always have more I want to say. That's when I know I'm on purpose.

When I visualize that scene that Mr. Canfield described, I relate to it. There is something about using my gifts and working in my calling that energizes me too. What energizes you? What do you feel driven to do, even if you're tired, that feeds your soul? What are the things that you show up for, no matter what?

Remember the previous chapter where I listed dream killers? If you have any dream killers within you, they will attempt to hinder you and keep you from showing up and stepping out. Remember, you have control over them, not the other way around, so decide to show up to your own calling!

Summary

God created us each with diverse gifts, and this diversity creates a unity and collaboration. How your calling shows up in the world depends on these factors:

1. The combination of your unique Calling Components™
2. The unique life message that God has you to share with others
3. The unique way you are to express yourself and to whom

There are many physical locations where God may call you to use your gifts, as well as in other environments, such as within relationships, in various modes of communication or on teams.

When it's time for you to *Step Out and Take Your Place,*
- Show up with confidence
- Show up with humility
- Show up knowing you've been provisioned
- Show up with love
- Just show up!

Operating in your calling will energize you, even when you feel like you have nothing left to give.

Prayer: *Thank You gracious Father. I rest in Your care. Thank You for the work You have called me to. Lord, help me to show up with humility,* *confidence and boldness, knowing that You are with me. I can step out and take the place that You've prepared for me. Help me be dedicated to the things of God and to the work You have for me to do.*

Ask yourself:

- What message has God given me to speak to the world?
- Am I a good steward of the blessings I already have?
- In what areas of my life do I feel confident in my own ability, and in which do I feel that my confidence is in God?

Affirmations:

I share my gifts with confidence.
I have a humble and contrite heart before the Lord.
When I show up ready with my gifts, amazing things happen.
Everywhere I go, my calling applies.

17.

Your Calling on Sunday

"Let us not become weary in doing good, for at the proper time
we will reap a harvest if we do not give up. Therefore, as we have
opportunity, let us do good to all people, especially to those who
belong to the family of believers." – Galatians 6:9-10 (NIV)

Do you attend a local church's weekend services? As His people, God tells us to fellowship and assemble with each other. You need people, and people need you. This time together encourages and strengthens our spirits as God works through our various gifts and callings.

"And let us consider one another in order to stir up love and good
works, not forsaking the assembling of ourselves together, as is the
manner of some, but exhorting one another, and so much the more
as you see the Day approaching." – Hebrews 10:24-25 (NKJV)

Your local church needs your help *very* much! It's appropriate to offer your skills, gifts and time to help out whenever possible. Serving in your local church is important and necessary for advancing the Kingdom of God, and is another vital reason to discover your gifts and calling. I won't spend a lot of time convincing you of this, as I believe you already understand the need to serve with your gifts. However, what you may not be aware of is this next question and its answer.

Are You Called to Ministry?

Yes.

Some of you are called to be part of a church staff or have a role as a pastor, teacher, apostle, prophet, or evangelist. When most of us hear the phrase, "called to the ministry," this is what we usually think of. Even if you're not called to these positions, you are still called to minister. *To minister means to give aid, offer service, support, comfort, or to care for.*

> To minister means to give aid, offer service, support, comfort, or to care for.

On a church staff or not, you still have the assignment to minister to others with your gifts at church.

I saw one pastor that appealed to his members to "please go from spectators to contributors." I believe this is God's will for us. Don't just fill a seat on Sunday morning. Contribute to the health of the body of Christ through your gifts and calling. What you have to offer makes a huge difference!

> *"Each of you should use whatever gift you have received to serve others, as faithful stewards of God's grace in its various forms. If anyone speaks, they should do so as one who speaks the very words of God. If anyone serves, they should do so with the strength God provides, so that in all things God may be praised through Jesus Christ. To him be the glory and the power for ever and ever. Amen."* – 1 Peter 4:10-11 (NIV)

At an author's event, I met a special person with a great personal story to tell. Author and speaker, Jason Frenn, is a missionary evangelist with the Assemblies of God fellowship of churches. His God-given calling is to officially minister the gospel to others, through crusades, foreign missions, radio shows, giving talks, etc. This is how he became aware of his calling:

When I walked onto the football field at Cal State University of Northridge, I had no idea what was about to hit me. All I knew was that my favorite music artist at the time was going to be one of the final acts of the three-day event. I had been a Christian for six months, and my knowledge of who's who in the religious world was limited to say the least. The fact that I was fifteen and came from a crazy family didn't help either.

I sat down on the grass with 500 other people and waited with great anticipation. The warm summer night was ideal for an open-air conference. After a short time of worship and praise, the first speaker walked to the podium. Up until that moment, the only two preachers I had heard of were Billy Graham and the Pope. But this man's voice thundered off the surrounding hills of the San Fernando Valley. His name was David Wilkerson. At the close of the message, I remember running to the altar and committing my life to whatever it was that he said we had to do.

The next morning, Jack Hayford spoke, and throughout the day great speakers such as Mario Murillo, and Dave Roever followed. Finally, the time came. My favorite singer made his way to the side of the flatbed trailer that served as a makeshift stage. The curly headed, bearded worship leader kissed his wife and walked up the stairs directly to the piano.

As he hammered out the first few notes to a song called Rushing Wind, I knew that God was orchestrating something that would mark my life forever. After a very memorable time of praise, he stood to his feet, walked over to the podium and opened his Bible.

"How many of you know for a fact that you are not called to the mission field?" He asked. In that crowd that grew to 1,000, about five people raised their hands. "Well, if you're wondering what the Bible has to say about the call of God on your life, you need not look any further. Jesus commands his disciples to go to the ends of the earth many times throughout the New Testament."

I didn't know how anyone else felt about that statement, but one thing was certain; God was talking to me. At that moment, I decided to become a missionary and dedicate my life to helping others find hope in Christ. Keith Green was the instrument God used that day to motivate me to step out and take my place on the mission field.

Was it easy? Of course not. I had to overcome a tremendous amount of adversities and obstacles. At first, my parents were not supportive of me going into ministry and eventually taking their grandchildren to Central America. My wife and I had to raise our budget during the recession of the early 90's, and I had to learn a foreign language. But was it worth it? Absolutely!

Since then, we have held more than fifty-three international crusades and have seen spoken to more than 3 million people and have seen more than 300,000 people make first-time decisions for Christ. I have spoken on Hour of Power many times and occasionally write for the Washington Post.

Each of us eventually comes to a point when God asks us to step out and take our place. When He does, you can count on the fact that He will make every provision, provide every open door, and give you above and beyond what you need to complete the task. Whether you feel called to be a missionary, a writer, business owner, doctor, pilot, mother, teacher or factory worker, God has something wonderful for you to accomplish in that area. If I can overcome the adversities of a crazy family plagued with nine divorces, alcoholism, and dysfunction, then just imagine what you can do with God's help!

At the young age of fifteen, Jason heard the call, accepted the call, and then worked towards the call. He has been called to church ministry and the mission field 24/7. Some of you will receive a similar assignment.

We're each called to minister to those around us on a daily basis as well. In the next chapter, this thought will be explored more. For now, let's stick to what you can do on Sundays. I'm going to ask you a series of questions to get you thinking about where your place is to serve others at your church.

- **What age group do you want to work with?**

Nearly all churches will offer programs and services for many age groups, such as children, teens, adults, and seniors. Who do you have a heart for?

- **Are you more comfortable in front of people, or doing behind the scenes work?**

Many churches have "behind the scenes" teams such as children's workers, youth group helpers, maintenance teams, database or file administrators, office support workers, volunteer coordinators, drivers, cooks, hospitality workers, decorators, small group/home group lesson writers, sound and light techs, parking attendants, event set-up/tear down, IT, etc.

Examples of "out front" roles include support group leaders, Sunday school teachers, worship team singers and musicians, ushers, greeters, pastors, special speakers, men's and women's ministry directors, youth group leaders, guest services, prayer team, etc.

- **Do you want to be involved with weekly service needs, or outreach activities?**

There are plenty of needs and roles to be filled within your church on a weekly basis. Just to get a weekend service prepared, it takes musicians, singers, sound and media techs, bulletin assembly, greeters, ushers, children's workers, a building cleaning and maintenance crew, prayer team, and many others.

Outreach activities are things like jail ministries, homeless programs, military fellowships, community service, missions, etc., that originate from your church, but take place outside of the church building.

- **Should you volunteer for any vacant role if there's a need, or only step into roles that match your calling and gifts?**

This is a great question that can bring up quite a debate! At times, I feel that both are valid, yet I want you to decide for yourself. Having said that, I know that each of us has a very specific role or place in the body of Christ. We see that in 1 Corinthians chapter 12.

> *"But now God has set the members, each one of them, in the body just as He pleased."* – 1 Corinthians 12:18 (NKJV)

If you are someone with the spiritual gift of "helps and serving," I suspect you might be able to jump right in anywhere, on almost any team, and feel great about what you're doing. Myself, I attend a larger church that has an abundant amount of opportunities to serve. It seems that there's something that fits everyone. I serve where my heart is; where my gifts and passions are. This works for me, as it helps me stay engaged and excited about what I'm doing. I know what I do to serve my church for weekend services is part of God's overall calling for my life.

This question brings up a larger question.

- **What happens if you find yourself serving in the wrong role/place at church, and/or you've lost your zeal for it?**

I've seen this happen several times. I know people personally who've struggled trying to make something work - a role that never fit them to begin with, or a role that has outgrown their capacity to manage it anymore.

During my book research phase when I interviewed pastors and church leaders, many of them brought up this issue as being a common problem. Being in the wrong role can cause team problems, dissatisfaction, hard feelings, and frustration that can cause people to be wary of serving again.

One time, I felt frustrated with a team leader, knowing inside that this team was being held back by their level of vision. The role was outgrowing their capacity to be in it, yet they were hanging on. I remember being in my car, asking God (more like complaining to God) why this person was still there, disagreeing with their decisions, and having other frustrated thoughts. He told me straight out, that it wasn't my business and He was dealing with it. From then on, I had a new attitude!

It's one thing to be in a role that you're supposed to be in, yet you feel ill-equipped or scared of it, and it's another to take a place that doesn't belong to you. I've done both of those in the past myself.

Typically, we aren't maliciously taking a place that doesn't belong to us. Usually, we're simply experimenting with where to serve, or someone else asks us to do it. The problem comes when we either;

- hang on to it, even when we know the right person for the role has arrived,
- when we are doing it poorly and cause problems, or
- when we really dislike it, but suffer through it anyway because we committed to it.

None of those situations represent how God wants us to be serving His people. It's detrimental for others and unhealthy for us. If you find yourself in this situation, and any or all of these bullet points apply to you, speak with your pastor. Express your heart to serve, but that you need to do so in the proper place that God designed you for. Also, have this conversation with the Lord to ask that His will be done.

> *"Defining your purpose will help you to determine the activities that you should be involved in. Like Jesus, you should not involve yourself in activities that contradict His purpose for your existence. Jesus' purpose was to do the will of the Father, and He never did anything contrary to that purpose. In the same way, your purpose should always be to do the will of the Father."* – Os Hillman

- **How involved are you able to be?**

OK, this is sort of a trick question. Really, it's better said, "How involved does God want you to be!" However, if you are going to step out at first in a modest way, it is something to think about.

Would you prefer a role that involves being part of teams with meetings during the week, or something that was weekend service only? Many volunteer teams have planning meetings or rehearsals in addition to weekend commitments. Other teams will require less time. Either way, ultimately serve where God wants you to.

For several years, I avoided joining the worship team at my church. Partially I was scared of the role, and the other issue was the time commitment it required. For quite a while, I was the sign language interpreter and interpreted all the music. I simply got the song list via email early in the week, then showed up five minutes before service on Sunday morning and took my place. By that time, the worship team had already been there practicing for ninety minutes.

Now, I look back and understand the importance of my interpreting experience. God is using it now in a powerful way for my calling. However, thankfully I was sensitive enough to serve at the next level when He opened the door for me to do so. I could have continued to say "no" to the commitment it required and missed a huge step along my journey. That step has led me here, to where I am today.

God has serving steps for you. At each step, He is preparing you for the next, which leads to your calling. It's like *you have a "calling road" rather than an exact destination.* When you're on it, you're in exactly the right place, heading in the right direction, in God's will for you.

> You have a "calling road" rather than an exact destination.

Matthew Klaus, a Church of God pastor in my community, says that we have a "serving sweet spot." It's the place where diligence, contentment, ownership, confidence, and no complaining happen. I pray that we all find our serving sweet spot, whether that means ministry as a vocation or serving the house of God for weekend services. Serving in your place of worship is definitely part of God's plan for you.

You help strengthen the body of Christ by bringing your unique gifts and calling to your church community.

Summary

God calls us to be members of the body of Christ. This includes gathering together with other believers, which usually includes weekend church services. Your gifts and calling are to be used in your local church. There are several initial questions you can use to self-assess what your best-fit role might be.

To minister means to give aid, offer service, support, comfort, or care for. You are called to minister at your church even if you're not on staff. You still minister to others through the sharing of your gifts at church.

With each servant/volunteer role you're in, God is preparing you for the next. You have "serving sweet spots" along the road of your calling; roles where you know you're in God's will for that season.

Prayer: *Great God, thank You that I can worship You freely in Your house every weekend. Giver of gifts, give me confirmation about the role You have for me, and help me be sensitive to Your Spirit. I want to take advantage of each step of preparation and every opportunity that comes from You Father. Allow me to see them when they show up and have the courage to step into them as You direct.*

Ask yourself:

- Where is my serving sweet spot?
- What is the role God has for me at church?
- Do I already know what role I should be in, but I'm avoiding it for some reason?

Affirmations:

I am called to ministry!
God is pleased to have me as a member of His body.
I am a faithful steward of God's grace.
I am on my calling road.

You are blessed with skills and gifts to be a blessing to others in the house of God. However, I know God doesn't want us to stop there. God's calling for you may also include the marketplace!

18.
Your Calling in the Marketplace

If there's one thing I'd like to impress upon you, it is this: You have special gifts and a God-driven purpose, and they're alive all day, every day, everywhere you go. Sundays, as well as Tuesdays and every other day of the week, you can shine forth to the world around you. If you want to do what you love, and love what you do, through God's leading, build a business, career or ministry on your giftings.

Outside of the walls of your church, your calling and God's purposes are alive and well.

In my network with Koinonia Business Women, I see the struggles that business owners and professional people have in the world of business. Often, Christians grapple with combining their spirituality and God-given gifts and purpose with their work. Yet at the same time, they deeply desire for their whole lives to be within God's will.

Take an honest look at these questions:

- Am I working my plan, or God's plan?
- Can I truly say my business brings value to the lives of others and uses my God-given gifts?
- Is my career's purpose or business' existence merely to make money?
- Am I settling for mediocrity and a comfort zone "box" rather than using my faith to make decisions and set goals?
- Do I section off my spiritual life, personal life and work life into separate segments that never or rarely intersect?
- Do I conduct myself in a way that shows Godly character in my career or business activities?
- Is there clarity of vision and purpose about what I am doing with my career or business, or am I just making stuff up as I go along?
- Have I taken the time to pursue God's heart about what my gifts are and how He wants me to use them in the world?

- Am I allowing fear (fear of failure, fear of what others will think, fear of success, self-doubts, fear of not having all the answers, fear of the unknown, etc.) to stop me from using my gifts in the marketplace?

I have experience with most of these struggles myself. I've also noticed another challenge for Christians and their work: Some business people work their businesses hard, but with little result, fruit and/or satisfaction. They are not sure the work they are doing is God's will or best for them. As God's people, we have the desire to know His plan and purpose for our lives and our work is a big part of that plan.

Another familiar struggle is when people separate their work or business lives from their spiritual lives, beliefs and principles. They have a "God box" and a "work box" and they never seem to intersect. As a believer, this is dangerous territory. Take this next story as an example. It's based on a true story of someone I used to know.

James has been a business owner for twelve years. He owns a construction company, and business has been slow in his area for about eighteen months. In the past, he's had the reputation of being a tough, demanding businessman, who at times has been difficult to work for or with. He chalks up his hard attitude to being a routine, "good business" practice.

About three years ago, he was introduced to the Bible and God by his sister, Patty. Since then, he's considered trying to soften his image, but hasn't seen the need to yet. He has kept God in the "God and church" box, and has continued to do business as usual.

As with most construction jobs, there are typically little things (or sometimes big things) that go wrong with each project. This one was no different. Unfortunately, something big went wrong.

At a job site, a city water pipe burst and ran for twenty-four hours before anyone noticed. It damaged landscaping and the dirt work on his work site, as well as caused flooding on a neighboring property. When the city came to inspect the pipes, they assumed it was a mistake made by the landscaping sub-contractor, and not the responsibility of James' company. The sub-contractor took responsibility for the problems, and planned to take care of all the repairs as soon as possible early the next week.

When James came to inspect it several hours later, he realized that was not the case. The burst pipe and the ensuing damage and flooding were, in fact, because of his own workers' mistake. It was Friday afternoon, and no one knew the truth except for him.

Over the weekend, he wrestled with integrity, and thoughts of self-preservation ran through his mind. "No one else knows we are responsible. I could say nothing and have the sub-contractor cover the costs. There are so many dishonest companies in this industry, so what's the big deal? Paying for this mistake will really hurt our profit level on this job. If I just keep my mouth shut, we could easily walk away from this responsibility and save some money. Business has been really bad lately, and we could use the cash. I am afraid for our company's future profitability. Admitting the mistake was ours might be humiliating and damaging to our image."

In between those self-serving thoughts, other thoughts like these also impressed themselves in his mind; "It's not the other sub-contractor's fault, and I would feel guilty making them pay for something they didn't do. God wants me to tell the truth. Pastor's sermon last Sunday was on doing the right thing, every time, even when we don't feel like it. No one else knows it's our fault, but God knows. I want to have a clean conscious. Can I live with myself if I cover this up? If I lie about this?"

As you can see, this was a huge situation in this business owner's life. He had to make a hard choice, and make no mistake; this choice was a critical spiritual decision.

Before, business was business. This situation would've been a no-brainer! Let it slide, and stick the sub-contractor with the bill. Now, James had the opportunity to apply Godly character to his vocation. On the level of character and integrity, will he now allow his faith and his business to intersect?

Why was he in this business? Did he value only what he can get for himself? Was it only for the money? Or does God have a plan for his gifts here, in ways that bring God's Kingdom to the earth? These are good questions, and the story continues…

When everyone returned to work after the long weekend, James presented the truth to everyone involved. After doing so, he felt a sense of freedom and release. Although it cost him for the repairs, it was worth every penny for a clean conscious and positive reputation. The other contractors and city workers were surprised and grateful for his honesty.

This whole situation was a test of James' integrity and character. Now he's shown himself to God as a person who will make the right decisions, and for this reason, can be trusted with more.

After this happened, God blessed James' business tremendously. In a time of economic downturn, James had plenty of business and new customers were referred to him. James' business was hiring, while many of his competitors were laying workers off.

My question is this: If he had chosen to be dishonest and lie to "save face" and save money, would he have been so blessed afterward? I doubt it. That decision and action would have been bad stewardship, and God cannot bless bad stewardship. Some may call it luck, but I don't believe in luck. Whatever we each sow, we also will reap. James sowed well.

Now it's time for James to take the intersection of faith and business to the next level. What if James were more proactive about making a difference in the lives of others through his business? How could he make a positive impact intentionally?

- Could he become a mentor?
- Create a non-profit section of his business to help the less fortunate?
- Donate a portion of his revenues from each home built to a charity of that customer's choosing?
- Use his skills and workers to help his church's building projects?
- Generously give offerings to ministries and charities out of the abundance of his business profits?

Sure! Any of those ideas, and scores of potential others would be wonderful ways to make a difference as a business person using your gifts.

> *"If you are going to discover how God wants to use your life and work, you must know why you were created. If you start trying to determine your purpose in life before understanding why you were created, you will inevitably get hung up on the things you do as the basis for fulfillment in your life, which will only lead to frustration and disappointment." – Os Hillman*

To back up for a moment, I'd like to expand my thoughts on this self-assessing question I posed before the story:

Am I allowing fear (fear of failure, fear of what others will think, fear of success, self-doubts, fear of not having all the answers, fear of the unknown, etc.) to stop me from using my gifts in the marketplace?

If we're honest, we can all acknowledge that fear is a battle we all fight in many areas of our lives. Fears of various kinds can easily stop us and our progress if we let them. When it comes to making decisions however, please remember this important piece of advice:

Nearly all spiritual, career, business, or relationship decisions that a person makes because of fear, will be the wrong decisions.

> *"Fear shows us the areas that we do not believe God for."* – Evangelist Ericka D. Jackson

Take the story of James for example. All of his reasons, excuses or justifications for not telling the truth were rooted in fear. "What will they think about our workmanship? Can we afford to pay for this mistake? Business is bad and I have a scarcity mindset."

> Nearly all spiritual, career, business, or relationship decisions that a person makes because of fear, will be the wrong decisions.

Do not be deceived, even by yourself. Fears lie to you about your future and potential. Fears also lie to you about whether or not God is All-Sufficient enough to provide, and tempts us to lean on our own understanding. Think about this:

- When you leave your God-given gifts on the table because of fear, you cheat yourself and those around you.
- When a person holds their gifts back, or remains unaware those gifts, that person's own destiny is stunted.
- The body of Christ remains weak when we lack gift awareness and use.

> Excuses about why you cannot share your gift are usually rooted in fear.

Excuses about why you cannot share your gift are usually rooted in fear.

> *"That's your stutter - that little thing that would rise up and excuse us from our destiny that happens to be what our stutter is, what our weakness is.*

171

That's our version of a Moses impersonation, by saying that "Well, I'm not qualified." The Bible says, "I will pour out my Spirit…." Nobody is exempt from what God wants to do in this hour." – Pastor Francis Frangipane

Now, let's talk more about your work. Aside from segmenting the aspects of our lives into boxes, or falling prey to fear, you may face another pitfall. As business owners, professionals or employees, a lot of people work for money, yet leave their God-given gifts and calling out of the picture.

Earlier in this book, I told the story of Katie and John, who spend their lives working at jobs having nothing to do with their gifts or talents. They feel stuck, dissatisfied and unhappy. I don't want you to have that same experience.

If you're already having that experience, don't beat yourself up about it. You're about to make some new moves. Trust me, there is hope! All that you've experienced, learned and done are assets which God can, and will, use for your future success. It has not been for nothing, and the wisdom and knowledge will not be wasted.

Think of your future as being a recipe. God has been positioning you into places where you can collect the ingredients, and all the pieces will come together into something useful.

This reminds me of my friend, Brian Jacks. He has an interesting story to share about how God is using his past experiences, jobs and skills, despite what appeared to be a career setback.

At age sixteen, I landed a job as teller for a major banking corporation. When I turned 18, I took the first of many promotions, and spent twenty years climbing the corporate ladder. As I progressed, I was beginning to realize my gifting with analytical and administrative type activities, and especially the ability to organize chaotic data into valuable information. On my off work hours, I did Kingdom work, such as serving on the board of an Assemblies of God church and became an important benefactor of two Christian schools in Peru.

During the first eighteen years with the bank, I loved my various jobs and could count on one hand the number of days I didn't want to go to work. I very much treated my employment as an opportunity to serve others, rather than serving myself for a paycheck. I told countless people over the years that if I had suddenly won the lottery, I would still go to work and that nothing in my life would change. I believe you need to operate in this mindset before true riches will be entrusted to you; otherwise, they will make wings and fly away.

My final two years with the corporation involved a very significant promotion, and I was catapulted into a position of high visibility. Throughout this period, I wasn't really enjoying my job like I had for my entire career up to that point. Clearly, God was trying to get me to learn something I would need for my future, but it wasn't comfortable as I was going through it.

Several significant personal events were also happening during this time period. My wife and I had reconciled from an almost certain divorce. We found a new church where I met my current pastor, Bill Krause. Pastor Krause offered to meet with me for one hour each week over a period of many months. It was to present a life coach/mentorship opportunity to develop both my faith and career potential. I had been sensing my career with banking was soon coming to an end and I was excited about this prospect, knowing beyond a shadow of a doubt it was the leading of the Lord.

A few months later, the end came. I negotiated with the bank for a fifteen-month fully paid severance package after twenty years of service. It was at this very moment my pastor pointed me in the direction of a revolutionary new business opportunity that I know will produce a significant personal and financial harvest in my life, thereby creating the ability to bless many people, businesses and ministries. I have also moved on to key roles within my church, in places where I can best utilize my natural God given talents, strengths and abilities. As an example, I recently coordinated two, three-day evangelistic crusades, and led a team of 100 volunteers (great leadership training for my new business).

It took me a long time to find out that the realm of God and realm of business could be interwoven, not separate boxes of my life. Many of the marketplace lessons I learned are the same skills needed for effective Kingdom work. Right now, I find myself working in a role before actually getting paid, which reminds me of the scripture that says, "If you are faithful with little, more will be added unto you." It's a worthy investment in my future, and I am sowing where I want to go.

It is so wonderful now to be functioning in the calling for which God has drawn me. Many people go through their lives like a fish out of water, flopping around in discomfort and frustration. But, when a fish is dropped into the water, its genius emerges, as the fish has the opportunity to flourish in its native environment. We each have a native environment. It's the one God has uniquely designed for our lives. When we operate in this flow, our genius emerges, as it connects with the guiding presence of the Holy Spirit. Operating any place else leaves a hole in our lives with much to be desired and many lost opportunities. This grand testimony in my life is just getting started...more to come.

Brian shared with me about how many of his past banking, management and technical skills he uses now both in the ministry, and in small business settings. I can almost guarantee that the experience that you're getting *right now* will somehow link together with your past and future experiences to aid your everyday calling.

Did you catch that? Right now, you are learning valuable things, in situations, relationships, ministry service, jobs, etc., that God can use to assist your life's calling.

It's good to have a job where you can use your gifts. When you do, you will;

- feel more satisfied,
- feel more appreciated,
- be more excited to go to work,
- have a sense of purpose,
- experience less frustration and weariness,
- bring more value to your workplace,
- be more confident about being in God's will, and
- know you are helping others in some meaningful way.

The last bullet point is important. God's calling on our lives always involves helping the lives of others in a meaningful way. You are called to some kind of work where this happens. Once you have your Calling Components™ defined (and understand more about how He has created you), and have awareness from God, you will better understand the kind of work He's calling you to. You'll also understand *where* God has called you to work; in an official ministry or in the marketplace. More on this in the next chapter.

Summary:

When we share our gifts through work, remember these important thoughts:

- Combine your faith and God's principles for life in your business and work, including actions and attitudes such as integrity, peace, love, and diligence.
- Recognize the places in your life where fear paralyzes you. Trust God, pray and do not lean on your own understanding. Making career and life decisions based on fear will be the wrong decisions. With God's help, you can overcome fears.
- If God leads you to a new career, business, ministry, or job that best utilizes your God-given gifts, move towards that goal with every life decision you make.
- God can use all of your work experience and skills to aid in His calling for you.

Prayer: *Lord God, thank You for working all around me. Your will be done in my life and work. I want to know and partner with Your purposes. You've called me to be a light in the world, but remind me that I'm not "of the world." Show me what I can do today to be operating in Your calling for me during my daily work. Lead me, always, in the right direction, to exactly where You want me to be.*

Ask Yourself:

- Do I section off my spiritual life, personal life and work life into separate segments that never or rarely intersect?
- Am I working just for the money, or am I using my gifts?
- How can I incorporate my faith into business and career decisions?

Affirmations:

My work brings glory to God.
God can use all of my past for His glory.
God is All-Sufficient and provides abundantly for me.

19.

Are You Called to Ministry or the Marketplace?

God assigns all of us some kind of work; some within a ministry organization, and some out in the world, or "marketplace." It is also possible that God may call you to both. The work that He has for you aligns with His heart for people. He wants to touch people's lives through you, in areas such as truth, justice, care, mercy, wisdom, peace, battle, salvation, provision, stewardship, healing, building up, tearing down, freedom, and love.

"Am I really a Kingdom worker if I'm not officially working in the ministry for a church?" Have you ever wondered that? You are not alone.

I've talked with so many people who feel like second-rate people of faith because in their mind, they're not doing God's work. Because they are not on staff at a church or running their own ministry, they wrestle with whether or not they're in God's will for their calling and work.

We're called to be salt and light in the world, and in the world but not of it. We're sent out into all industries, business sectors, government agencies, city services, educational settings, entrepreneurship, factories, and in entertainment. Why? God places and positions us everywhere for His purposes. He needs His people everywhere.

If God's calling for you includes having a regular job or owning a business, fabulous! You can still serve at your local church on the weekends as God directs you to. Think about how many biblical saints served God's purposes while working regular jobs! Also, remember that God uses those who earn income in the marketplace to bring finances into the church.

Next, I've included a couple personal stories from friends in my business network. See if you can identify with their journeys - journeys that have brought them to the place of feeling confident in God's will for their lives.

The first story I'd like you to read is from author Os Hillman. He and I have a similar calling from the Lord, focusing on helping God's people understand His calling for their lives. He specifically focuses on marketplace callings, and has founded an organization called Marketplace Leaders Ministries. Here is his story:

I believe most of us will experience many jobs and experiences on our way to discovering the purpose or destiny for which God made us. For some of us, that destiny will not be an event or a specific thing, but a process over our lifetime. I discovered my purpose late in life. I grew up thinking that my destiny was to be the next Jack Nicklaus.

When I was eleven years old, my dad encouraged me greatly in playing golf. I eventually became a very good junior player and even received a golf scholarship to the University of South Carolina. I thought I was well on my way to becoming a professional golfer on the PGA Tour; but when I finished school and turned pro, I quickly grew frustrated and disillusioned with my inability to get to a level to play competitively as a professional.

As the years went by, I decided that golf was no longer the profession I felt God wanted me to be in. I made a career change into sales and marketing, but after being in various jobs for six years, I found myself longing to grow more in the Lord and serve Him in a greater capacity. I was involved in starting a church with two other men who were seeking to be used by God. "Perhaps I am really called to be a pastor," I thought to myself. I decided to take a leave of absence from my job and go to a three-month Bible study course. I then decided to move to Atlanta to serve as an assistant pastor, only to have the position removed after three months. This caused me to go back into the business world. In hindsight, I see that this was the hand of God.

Through it all, I learned that I was never cut out to be a pastor or to have a "vocational ministry;" I was designed to be in business. On the other hand, I could not help but think of myself as a "second-class" Christian who was not quite sold out to the purposes of God. I don't believe that anyone was saying this to me; it was more implied by the Christian culture around me.

Next, I met a woman who specialized in working with executives in career transition. She helped people understand their core purpose in life from God's perspective, and she challenged me to go through this process. At the end of a tiresome day, we came up with this statement: The purpose for which God made Os Hillman is to articulate and shepherd foundational ideas for transformation.

The interesting thing is that my core purpose had been modeled already while a golf professional, a business consultant and an advertising agency owner. I had "articulated and shepherded" ideas in these arenas. Today God is doing it in a spiritual way through writing, mentoring and leading a movement to help people understand their work as a calling.

Right now, Os works in the world of business where he is ministering to people at the same time. Wonderful!

The next story is from one of my mentors, Steve Harrison, who runs a very successful author PR and marketing business with his brother, Bill. Many best-selling authors credit Steve and Bill as being the catalyst for their success. As a Christian man in business, Steve has also wrestled in the past with whether or not he was in God's will; if he was really where God wanted him to be in his life and work.

As with many of us, *we desire to be "doing the Lord's work," but have a difficult time reconciling the fact that we actually are, outside of the walls of our churches.*

When Steve and I talked about God's gifts and calling, I asked him what his experiences have been in discovering his everyday calling. He offered this story about his experiences.

> We desire to be "doing the Lord's work," but have a difficult time reconciling the fact that we actually are, outside of the walls of our churches.

I know that God is the One Who sees me.

> *"You are the God who sees me," for she said, "I have now seen the One who sees me." – Genesis 16:13b (NIV)*

From about age twenty on, I always thought about going into the ministry. I felt like I had (and have) a lot of talents for that, but there was always something holding me back. On one level, I was interested, but then can't say that God was really calling me to it either. I said to myself, "I could be good at this, but I really enjoy sales; I enjoy marketing and helping people in that way. Do I want to be a minister?"

About two years after God saved our company from the brink of bankruptcy, I was doing a publicity summit seminar for authors. A participant came up to me and said, "You know, I felt like I was hearing from a pastor. In fact, I felt like I was hearing from a pastor talking to other pastors." On a different occasion, I had another woman say, "Well it's a good thing you didn't go into the ministry. We need you here." Those are just a couple of the many confirmations that I am on the right path.

Many of us ask, "How can I do what I'm gifted at doing?" It's not first and foremost about what I do or even where I am, but who I am in Christ. I don't think Paul wanted to be in prison. He had dynamic gifts. Paul probably had every right to say, "Why should I be stuck in this prison?" Yet, were it not for those circumstances, we wouldn't have a lot of the scripture that we now have.

One of the first sermons I heard my pastor speak talked about blooming where you are planted. The other day as I wrote in my journal, I felt like the Lord was telling me to stop trying to prove myself. Yes, my mind still thinks about doing more, achieving certain projects and different kinds of work, all while loving what I am doing, but I am more aware now that it really is about blooming where you're planted, using gifts, etc.

We often think that by getting a new job or a new set of circumstances will be "it." Satan sometimes shows us a false road, rather than the road of the cross. We're called to pick up a cross. In this day and age, there are SO many things you could do. That is the good news, and the bad news. Just because you could do something, doesn't mean you should. If a door opens for something, pray about it.

Although I didn't go into the ministry, I really can be a minister through my business. My brother likes to use this quote, "Preach the gospel at all times, and only when necessary open your mouth." Through my work, I encourage and advise people to follow their calling and use their gifts. When I help them get the word out, I'm helping save marriages; I'm helping people lose weight; I can help someone get out of foreclosure by helping authors help them.

I get confirmation every day that I am in His will, because God saved my business, because I make a difference in the lives of the people I assist, because I enjoy the work, and because it seems effortless and the ideas come easy. There is a sense that I am wired for this; that God has made me for this work where I can bless people. I'm seeing fruit. Looking for where God is at work is so critically important for us as disciples.

As you can see, Os and Steve make a big impact on people's lives. They use their gifts well and are excited and content with the work God has called them to. God has prepared a special work for you, in advance, that serves His purposes. It may be in the marketplace!

Wherever God positions you, according to His calling, it's where you need to be. There's no need to compare your calling to the callings of others. Remember, there is divine unity established in our diversity. Discover your special place and embrace it.

Summary

God calls many of His people to the marketplace. He needs His people positioned in every industry, workplace, government sector, educational system, etc. When we are, His purposes can be served in those places. Consider how many biblical saints worked in marketplace trades and jobs.

If you've ever struggled with feelings of insecurity as a Christian in the marketplace, you're not alone. Some people have felt like they were not doing the "Lord's work" if they weren't working for a ministry organization. This is simply not true. Seek Him and become confident about His calling for you. He sends many of us out into the marketplace to serve His purposes there, and that is great!

Prayer: *Mighty God, You are great! Thank You for the provision You supply me with. You are my Provider. May I always glorify You and serve Your purposes through my work. If You've called me to the marketplace, let me be secure and confident in Your will for me in my marketplace work. Send me out while holding me in the palm of Your hand.*

Ask yourself:

- Am I called to ministry in church, in the marketplace or both?
- In what way does my work serve God's purposes and impact the lives of others?
- Do I feel concerned that I am not doing the Lord's work because I have a marketplace job?

Affirmations:

I am called to ministry!
God is pleased to have me as a member of His body.
I am a faithful steward of God's grace.
My work makes a difference.

20.

God Has Something to Say, To You & Through You

"Also I heard the voice of the Lord, saying: "Whom shall I send, and who will go for Us?"

Then I said, "Here am I! Send me."

And He said, "Go, and tell this people…" – Isaiah 6:8-9a (NASB)

Have you ever seen those New Year's confetti-popper toys? They're small, bottle-shaped containers with a string, and when you pull the string, an assortment of colorful streamers and confetti explodes out. When I think about what the Lord has given each of us, I get a fun visual. Imagine this:

As God is forming us in our mothers' wombs, He creates a special confetti box for each person. Inside, is a variety of gifts, talents, skills, abilities, interests, passions, future plans, personality, etc.; a variety of unique characteristics, all wrapped up in a box that represents His purposes.

He gives us our confetti box and waits for us to mature and discover that it's from Him, and that it contains amazing things. Since it's wrapped in His purposes, some people ignore the box, never opening it. Others stare at it, afraid to open it, for fear of what's inside.

A select group of His people will take hold of the box, venturing out into uncharted territory. This is you. You know it's a box from God, and are certain that what's inside is magnificent.

As you pull the string to open it, the contents burst out, filling the air with blessings; encompassing you, your surroundings, everyone and everything nearby. The shimmer lingers, drifting and swirling, landing exactly where God commands it to; touching the lives of many.

Can you see it? What God has given you was meant to be discovered, opened and shared. God Himself designed the contents, and they serve His purposes. He sows a message, it grows and changes your life, and then it comes out of you to influence others.

Krista Dunk

Administering your gifts is ministering. By doing so, you minister a message to others, right from the Lord's heart.

Here is a special equation for you:

**Using your gifts and abilities +
Sharing a specific message and/or helpful action as God directs
= Calling (or mission in life)**

Your gifts and abilities (in your confetti box) include the Calling Component™ items found in chapter 7. These are the ways in which God has created you; your unique make up.

The specific message or helpful action God wants you to convey can also be found within your Calling Component™ items; specifically within your past experiences and passions. It may also be found in any Rhema words or visions the Lord has spoken to you directly. Because of what you've been through, experienced, overcome, been divinely given, etc., you have a special authority to convey this message to others.

This "work, calling or mission" that God has for your life will always help other people's lives in some meaningful way.

> This "work, calling or mission" that God has for your life will always help other people's lives in some meaningful way.

What are the messages God wants to speak to people? He has all kinds of messages for *all* kinds of people. For example, here are some of the things God wants to communicate:

Faith	Wisdom	Tearing Down
Hope	Growth	Strongholds
Love	Leadership	Creative Power
Salvation	Servanthood	Worship
Freedom	Purity	Commitment
Expression	Grace	Legacy
Humility	Mercy	Christlikeness
Justice	Power	Government
Truth	Beauty	Repentance
Forgiveness	Overcoming	Safety
Healing	Peace	Stewardship
Building Up	Discipline	Value
Refining	Stirring Up	

Dozens more messages could be added to this list, all of which are related to what God wants to accomplish in the world and in individuals' lives. His messages draw people to Him, to His truth and to His love. He partners with you and me to accomplish His plan!

How you share the message depends on the abilities and capacities that God has placed in you, as well as *who* the message is to.

The "how" of communicating the message could include any of these modes:

- Speaking
- Writing
- Creative Arts
- Serving/Helping Hands
- Demonstrating

Take note of the communication methods that come naturally to you. However, like with my public speaking example, you may have the capacity to communicate in a way that you aren't using yet. God knows!

The "who" is the group, or groups, of people who need to hear the message God has given you to convey. This group of people will see you as someone who knows what they're going through because you've been there yourself. They can relate to you, or look to you as a source for answers or help. You have credibility with them, and they may be more open to hear what you have to say.

Your "who group" depends on who you have a heart for, and who needs the message the most. God will show you who they are. Examples of people groups that God might call you to help and influence are:

Aspiring business owners	Soldiers with PTSD
Single parents	Orphans in a foreign country
Young married couples	Teens with poor self-images
Toddlers	Kids with ADHD
Women of God	Hispanic men
Political leaders	Deaf high school students
Homeless families	Homeschooling moms
Victims of domestic violence	Youth group pastors
People in jail	Cancer patients
Church leaders in third-world countries	Recovering addicts or alcoholics
Lonely seniors	Foster children
Men or women who've been abused	Idle believers

Let me use my calling as an example of how this all works together:

My Core Calling: ***To Build up the body of Christ (expression*)***

Message #1: Discover calling and gifts so the body of Christ can be strengthened
Message #2: Creative expression in worship/freedom in expressive worship

How #1: Speak and write
How #2: Demonstrate through creative arts

Group #1: God's people who desire God's plan and will for their lives, and business women
Group #2: God's people open to going deeper in their worship experience, and those with an interest in sign language

*Expression is a key word in my calling. I help people express their hearts to God in worship through demonstrating the combination of worship music, sign language and dance (also by teaching others how to worship with sign themselves). Another aspect of helping people with "expression" is giving people the tools and how-to path for discovering their calling and gifts. This also helps people express the core of who they are as an act of worship to God, and as an act of service to others.

At some point, you will have a clear representation like this of your calling too. You may want to create a page for yourself with an outline like the one above, even if it's blank for now. Include your Calling Components™ there too, as they facilitate your calling.

I know my calling now. However, a year from now it won't look exactly the same as it does today. It's ever-growing and evolving. Once that calling path is discovered, our job is to listen to God and obey His leading along the path.

Your Calling Will Become Your "New Normal"

The more you use your gifts and operate in your calling, the more you get used to being an instrument in God's hand. The concept of stepping out to take your place may seem challenging or make you feel uneasy now, but rest assured, it will become your "new normal." Operating in your calling and using your gifts will become an everyday activity.

This is an exciting time for you. Just like the story of learning to ride a bike, we ride along our calling path mastering each phase as it comes. Ride on - Open that box! It's Time to *Step Out and Take Your Place!*

Summary

Your "work, calling or mission" from God will always help other people's lives in some meaningful way. God sows into you a message, it grows, and then it comes out of you to influence others. By doing so, you minister a message to others, right from the Lord's heart.

Using your gifts and abilities + Sharing a specific message and/ or helpful action as God directs = Calling (or mission in life)

The "how" of communicating the message God wants you to convey could include any of these modes:

- Speaking
- Writing
- Creative Arts
- Serving/Helping Hands
- Demonstrating

Who you're supposed to convey it to is the group, or groups, of people who most need to hear the message God has given you. God will show you who you're called to influence and share with.

Even though your calling evolves and grows, at some point operating in your calling will become your "new normal." This is an exciting time for you!

Prayer: *Loving God, You are wonderful! Thank You for Your faithfulness to me. Lord, I want what You've given me to explode out and bless others. It blesses me just to know that You love me so much, and have designed me to serve Your purposes. Give me wisdom, strength and boldness to take hold of my calling.*

Ask yourself:

- What will keep me motivated to continue with this discovery journey?
- What have I been trying to do in my own strength?
- Can I define the message God wants to convey to others through me yet? If so, what is it?

Affirmations:

God has given me fabulous gifts!
My gifts serve God's purposes on the earth.
I trust the Lord, and I know He uses me to make a difference in the lives of others.

Conclusion & Next Steps

"For God's gifts and his call are irrevocable." – Romans 11:29 (NIV)

Your gifts are for God's glory. Your calling is for God's purposes. Your time to discover them is now.

As you've been on this journey, maybe you're starting to realize that you've been sharing some of your gifts already, but weren't aware of it. Maybe you're seeing that you're already operating in your calling in small ways. Either that or you've become aware of sweeping life changes that are needed so that you can align with God's plan for you. Whatever the case may be, your calling journey does not end until you reach the gates of Heaven, and it may even apply there too!

Looking back, you may see that you've tried a lot of things in your past as you've searched for your life's calling and purpose. Many of us have wasted a lot of time trying to carry out our own plans. Do not dismay! God can use everything from your past surrendered to Him, and from now on you can live life purposefully. This verse is a powerful thought:

> *"Many are the plans in a man's heart, but it is the LORD's*
> *purpose that prevails."* – Proverbs 19:21 (NIV)

Thankfully, now you have new, valuable information about the Lord's plan for your life. What we attempt to accomplish in our own strength does not produce much fruit. However, since the Lord's purpose is what prevails, and our gifts play a role in His purposes, that's exciting news for your future. There is freedom for your soul within God's plan!

> *"Then you will know the truth, and the truth*
> *will set you free."* – John 8:32 (NIV)

Important thoughts for you to remember:

- *God does not require perfection for service.*
- *One way that you share God's love and light is through using your unique set of gifts.*
- *Purpose is alive, relentlessly.*
- *People are waiting to be influenced by you, inspired by you, taught by you, helped by you, loved by you.*
- *What is my personal potential?*
- *Become confident in your call, and celebrate the call of others.*
- *The "new you" starts in your mind and heart through the revelation God gives you.*
- *Without a mindset that tells you that you can, you won't.*
- *We are meant to become more and more like Jesus as we spiritually mature.*
- *If you want what God wants for your life, you will need to think what God thinks about your life.*
- *If you aren't planning to succeed, what are you planning to do?*
- *To carry out our calling in life, as God desires, we need to show up with a spirit of love.*
- *Allow yourself to be you, as a leader.*
- *You are called to minister with your life, seven days a week.*
- *Nearly all spiritual, career, business, or relationship decisions that a person makes because of fear, will be the wrong decisions.*
- *This "work, calling or mission" that God has for your life will always help other people's lives in some meaningful way.*

Here are some next steps for your journey that you can take today:

- **Keep This Book Open**

Have you noticed in life, that you pay attention to the things that are in front of your face? I encourage you to keep this book open. It's a lot to take in all in one read, and different sections will apply to different time periods of your journey. Work one piece at a time. Come back to it often.

- **Do the Inner and Outer Work**

Return to The Gift Discovery Cycle™, Spiritual Gifts, Calling Components™ and Discovery Strategy chapters. The inner and outer work ideas revealed are here to benefit your life if you will take the time to pursue them. Along the way, you'll notice a deeper relationship forming with God. It is through that relationship that the revelation of who were created to be comes.

Without a doubt, time termites, distraction and dream killers will try to stop your progress. Instead, stay dedicated to it. If you desire God's best and will for your life (and those for whose lives you will touch), taking this journey of discovery is one of the most important endeavors you will ever undergo. You will prevail!

- **Share Your Journey with Someone Else**

Who can you share this journey with? Do you have a close friend, family member or mentor who supports your spiritual and personal growth? Invite them to go on the journey to discover and live their calling as well. Form a small group of like-minded people who can work through this and encourage each other along the way. At the very least, have someone who you can talk to, who will keep you accountable to your goals and will check in on your progress. A little bit of encouragement goes a long way.

- **Document Your Journey**

I am so excited for you! I can just imagine the "ah-ha" moments you'll have, and all the new information you'll get that's teeming with revelation about who God has created you to be. Trust me, you'll without a doubt desire to capture all of this amazing information. But how? Maybe one of these ideas would work for you: A journal, blog, diary, computer document, video log, an audio journal, a vision board. I prefer a written journal, so that I can keep everything in one place. And, there are times when I believe that my written handwriting captures the emotion of the moment.

Whatever you choose, be sure to document your calling discovery journey.

- **Get the *Step Out and Take Your Place Companion Workbook***

Another great way to document your progress is to use the workbook that corresponds with this book. The workbook offers more questions and exercises that correspond with each chapter. It includes a full-sized ME CHART™ to use for your Calling Components™, and other fill-in-the-blank sections. It's available in e-book version and printed booklet.

Please visit the Resources Section for full details.

- **Practice Gratefulness**

Maybe you have a long way to go on your journey to discover your calling. Be okay with that. Where you are at right now is not where you'll stay, nor is it where you've been. Give God thanks for sustaining you. Thank Him ahead of time for the answers He will provide. Be thankful for the blessings you already have. I believe that God draws near to a grateful, thankful person.

- *Step Out and Take Your Place*

God will continue to ask you to step forward, from one "place" to the next "place" on your designated calling path. You're on your way to living the life God has for you! If you persevere with this journey, you *will* discover and live your everyday calling. After all, you are His workmanship, created in Christ Jesus for good works, which God prepared beforehand that you should walk in them. Amen!

> *"For the LORD your God will bless you in all your harvest and in all the work of your hands, and your joy will be complete."* – Deuteronomy 16:15b (NIV)

My Prayer for You:

You are worthy, Wonderful Counselor! May Your purposes endure through all generations and within my new friend. Help this reader know You more. Give them opportunities for the exact kind of learning that they need, right now. I pray that they will cherish the gifts You've generously given them, and will choose to be a good steward of these gifts. We avail ourselves to Your righteous plan, and we want to take our places within Your purposes. Help my new friend to be bold and confident in You as they step out and take their place, and bless them with Your presence. In Jesus' name. Amen.

Resources

Salvation Prayer:

If you've never prayed to God, asking Him for forgiveness of sins, and confessing that you believe Jesus His son was crucified as payment for your sins, you can do so right now. Ask Jesus to become the Lord of your life, and for the salvation that He freely offers to all who believe in Him. If you believe it in your heart, say this out loud (or your own version of it):

Father God, I believe in You and Your plan. You made me for Your purposes. I want to know You more, and become who You want me to be. Please forgive my sins, as I have fallen short in many areas of my life. You know all my weaknesses. I believe that You sent Jesus Christ, Your Son, to die on a cross to cover my sins. I receive Your free gift of salvation through what Jesus did for me. Help me Lord! Send Your Spirit to live within me and fill me with Your wisdom. Thank You that You've adopted me into Your Kingdom. For Yours is the Kingdom, and the power and the glory, forever. Thank You Father, in Jesus' name!

> *"...the Son of Man [Jesus] be lifted up, that whoever believes in Him should not perish but have eternal life. For God so loved the world that He gave His only begotten Son, that whoever believes in Him should not perish but have everlasting life. For God did not send His Son into the world to condemn the world, but that the world through Him might be saved. "He who believes in Him is not condemned; but he who does not believe is condemned already, because he has not believed in the name of the only begotten Son of God."* – John 3:14b-18 (NKJV)

Contributors:

Jevon Bolden
Developmental Book Editor, Praise and Worship Leader
Orlando, Florida
www.EmbraceTheImpossible.blogspot.com

Jack Canfield
Co-Author of the *Chicken Soup for the Soul* series, author of *The Success Principles*
Founder of The Canfield Training Group - Santa Barbara, California
www.JackCanfield.com

Gail E. Dudley
Pastor's wife, Ministry in Motion Servant Leader, Columbus, Ohio
Author of *Ready to Pray Workbook: A Spiritual Journey of Prayer and Worship*
www.mimtoday.com/booksbygail.html

Pastor Trisha Ferguson
Praise and Worship Pastor, business owner
Olympia, Washington
www.Go2CCC.org, www.IRCprint.com

Pastor Francis Frangipane
Advancing Church Ministries, Author of *The Three Battlegrounds* (Cedar Rapids, IA: Arrow Publications, 1989) and *I Will Be Found By You*
Cedar Rapids, Iowa
www.Frangipane.org

Pastor Ray Frederick
Capital Christian Center, Olympia
Shelton, Washington
www.Go2CCC.org

Jason Frenn
Missionary, Evangelist, Author of *Power to Reinvent Yourself* and *Breaking the Barriers*
Irvine, California
www.Frenn.org

Steve Harrison
Bradley Communications Corp., RTIR
Philadelphia, Pennsylvania
www.ReporterConnection.com

Teri Hawkins
International Speaker, Bestselling Author, Founder of the Savvy
Entrepreneur Club
Bend, Oregon
www.SavvyEntrepreneurClub.com

Os Hillman
Author of *TGIF – Today God is First*, Founder of Marketplace Leaders
Ministries
Cumming, Georgia
www.MarketplaceLeaders.org

Evangelist Qaiser Ijaz
Passion of Christ Ministries
Pakistan
http://PassionofChrist.weebly.com

Brian Jacks
Sacramento, California
www.SacramentoInsights.com

Dr. Noreen Jacks
Bible scholar and teacher, Author of *Promises from the Olive Tree*
Woodland, California
www.NoreenJacks.com

Nicole Kirksey
Certified Life and Leadership Coach, Chief Visionary Officer of
Foundational Gifts
Hershey, Pennsylvania
www.FoundationalGifts.com

Derrick "The Encourager" Miles
Author of the *Super Human Performance* series
Raleigh, North Carolina
www.MilestoneMotivation.com

Dr. Rick D. Miller
Certified Counselor, ARNO Profile System™ test administrator
Cannon Beach, Oregon
www.CrisisConsultingNW.com

Senior Pastor Dave Minton
Capital Christian Center, leadership mentor
Olympia, Washington
www.Go2CCC.org

Tammy "The Word Cop" Redmon
Certified Executive Team Coach
Olympia, Washington
www.TammyRedmon.com

Dondi Scumaci
Author of the *Designed for Success* series, corporate executive team mentor
Austin, Texas
www.DondiScumaci.com

Marnie Swedberg
Mentor to Super Busy Women
Warroad, Minnesota
www.Marnie.com | 877-77-HOW-TO

First Lady Tomekia Williams
Life Church of Jacksonville
Jacksonville, Florida
www.ACityofLife.com

Resources:

Adoption
Ibsen Adoption Agency – www.IbsenAdoptionNetwork.com

Business Organizations
Koinonia Business Women – www.KBWomen.com

Marketplace Leadership Institute – www.MarketplaceLeaders.org

Fasting
Jentezen Franklin Ministries – www.JentezenFranklin.org/fasting

Journaling
Lois Williams, Author
Love Letters From Lois
www.LoveLettersFromLois.com

Order a *Gifts & Calling Discovery Journal*
www.StepOutandTakeYourPlace.com

Prayer
Gail E. Dudley
Pastor's wife, Ministry in Motion Servant Leader
Author of *Ready to Pray Workbook: A Spiritual Journey of Prayer and Worship*
www.mimtoday.com/booksbygail.html

Margaret Agard
Author of *In His Footsteps: How to Be Happy Soul Deep*
www.InHisFootsteps.com

A community of hope and encouragement - www.TheWallofPrayer.com

Spiritual Warfare/Battles
Book: *Beyond Fearless – How to Remove Every Hindrance From Your Life,*
by Ericka D. Jackson. www.ErickaJackson.com

Book: *Battlefield of the Mind, by Joyce Meyer.* www.JoyceMeyer.org

Book: *Know Thine Enemy – A Guide to Intelligent Deception,* by C. A.
Huft. www.ChristianParanormalAnswers.com

Tests & Assessments
Marketplace Gifts Assessment: www.MilestoneMotivation.com/gifts

www.LiveCareer.com

The Path Elements Profile™: The Profile that 'Gets People.'
www.lauriebethjones.com
www.lauriebethjones.com/store/PEP-Products.html

ARNO Profile System™ – Dr. Rick Miller, test administrator – www.
CrisisConsultingNW.com

Spiritual Gifts Tests:
www.bibleistrue.com/sgtest/testa.htm
www.kodachrome.org/spiritgift/
www.buildingchurch.net/g2s-i.htm

Secular Book: *Journey to You*, by Steve Olsher – "The Seven Seeds of Your Soul" tool, chapter 15. www.SteveOlsher.com

Worship
Trisha Ferguson, Worship Pastor - www.Go2CCC.org

Learn to worship with sign language - www.WorshipWithSign.com

Want More Step Out and Take Your Place (SOTYP) Resources & Links?

Companion Workbook:

Order your copy of the *Step Out and Take Your Place Companion Workbook* online now at www.StepOutandTakeYourPlace.com. Available in eBook version (immediately downloadable) and printed booklet (sent via USPS mail).

Free Email Newsletter:

Sign up for the free "Gifts & Calling (email) Newsletter" at www.StepOutandTakeYourPlace.com today for tips and inspiration to help you stay on track with your journey.

Small Group Study System:

Are you interested in having your small group, business team, home group, Bible study, full congregation, or women's fellowship take the *Step Out and Take Your Place* journey together?

Visit www.StepOutandTakeYourPlace.com to learn more about the Small Group Study System. Quantity discounts available.

Audio Book – Special Offer:

As a special offer to purchasers of this book, you can order the *Step Out and Take Your Place* audio book on CD for just $5.50, including shipping. Or, opt for downloadable audio files for just $3. Visit this exclusive webpage (just for you) to order: www.StepOutandTakeYourPlace.com/audiodeal.htm.

Virtual Workshop:

Learn more about Krista's SOTYP Virtual Workshop held once a quarter. You can participate from anywhere, and receive more personalized help and teaching. Visit the workshop page at www.StepOutandTakeYourPlace.com for more information.

- Follow Krista on Twitter: www.Twitter.com/GiftsandCalling (Hash Tag #SOTYP)
- Contact Krista to speak at your upcoming event or to host a virtual workshop for your group: www.KristaDunk.com

©2011 - Step Out and Take Your Place/Krista Dunk

About the Author

Author and speaker Krista Dunk is the co-founder of Koinonia Business Women, an organization for businesswomen of faith. Krista has taken a personal journey with God to discover His calling and unique gifts for her life, and is now using this journey to mentor others. Her dream is to see all of God's people discover, develop, and share their gifts effectively so that the body of Christ is strengthened and God's purposes are fulfilled. While writing Step Out and Take Your Place, Krista surveyed and interviewed pastors, women's ministry directors, counselors, business owners, and people of faith about their struggles, feedback, experiences, and needs in this area of spiritual growth.

Besides her writing, speaking, and entrepreneurial adventures, Krista is also a wife, mother, sign language interpreter, worship team member, and small-group leader with her husband at their local church in Olympia, Washington.

CPSIA information can be obtained at www.ICGtesting.com
262101BV00002B/2/P